Prep School Days
The Seminary at the University of Notre Dame

by

ANDREW STEVANS

"I applaud the work of Andrew Stevans to celebrate the fine, whole-person education provided by the Congregation of Holy Cross at its Prep Seminary ("The Little Sem") on the Notre Dame campus. Many of my colleagues in Holy Cross speak with great affection of their days there and of the committed religious who prepared them so well for life and ministry. These are stories that need to be told."

Edward A. "Monk" Malloy, C.S.C.,
President Emeritus, University of Notre Dame

Prep School Days
The Seminary at the University of Notre Dame
© Andrew L. Stevans 2011

All Rights Reserved

No portion of this publication may be reproduced, stored in any electronic system, or transmitted in any form or by any means, electronic, mechanical, photocopy, recording, or otherwise, without the written permission from the author. Brief quotations may be used in literary reviews.

ISBN: **978-0-9848340-0-6**

Library of Congress Control Number (LCCN): **2011961681**

For Information Contact
P.O. Box 613, Merrifield, VA 22116-0613

Printed in the USA by CreateSpace
7290 Investment Drive, Suite B
North Charleston, SC 29418

8.5" x 11" (Paperback edition): Morris Publishing, USA
3212 East Highway 30, Kearney, NE 68847

CONTENTS
--INTRODUCTION... vi
--MAP: HOLY CROSS AT NOTRE DAME... viii

AUGUST ARRIVAL AT HOLY CROSS
Notre Dame, Indiana: Holy Cross Preparatory Seminary... 1
The Melon Patch... 3
Fishing with Davis; The Tackle Box... 7
Kohlerman House... 9
Painting Lockers with De Lawd... 11
 --Making and Unmaking Beds
 --Catching Muskrats
 --Photographing the Swans; Lake Debris
Mortier, Monitor, Lineman... 16
The Tower Hill Incident... 18

...SOPHOMORE YEAR...
Meeting Classmates... 23
Visiting Fr. Fiedler... 25
Four-Part, A Cappella Choir... 30
Latin & Lumberjacks... 33
The Race Around St. Joe's Lake... 37
Steam Men... 41
Ice Man, Funnyman... 46
Parents: Visiting Sundays... 48
The Soiree... 52

...JUNIOR YEAR...
-CSMC... 57
Walking Wounded: The Junior Senior Game... 58
Sr. St. Rita's Dispensery... 61
Quarentined... 65
Kitchen Support; the Grease Trap... 68
Spud Kings... 71
Eating Wild Venison... 73
Musicals, Holy Cross Style... 75
Fr. Ed Shea, Mr. Cody and French Lecons... 79
 --Teaching Latin
Father William Lyons' History... 83
Fr Dean O'Donnell's English Class... 85
The Unofficial Football Kicking Contest... 88

Locker Room Invasion... 91
Roger Sowala... 92

...SENIOR YEAR...
Sixteen-Inch Ball: Passing a Dangerous Summer's Eve... 94
Hockey, Football, Basketball, Baseball... 97
  --Hockey
  --Zero Degrees Fahrenheit
  --Football
  --Basketball
  --Baseball
Sr. Life Saving, Swimming—and Wading... 106
  --Wading in Juday Creek
  --Senior Life Saving
  --Swimming at Pinhook Lake
Father Simmons and Greek Class... 110
Roommates, Bell Ringing and Fr, Brinker's Physics Class... 113
Homicide Detective... 116
Halloween: Refectory... 118
Reader and Priest Waiter... 122
St. Mary's College, Sand Pits and Science Fiction... 125
"Spring Cleaning:" St. Mary's Lake...127
Washing, Waxing and Squeegee-ing... 129
Field Day... 132

...POST HOLY CROSS YEARS...
Holy Cross Graduation; The Summer of 1955... 135
    --Bay City Michigan
    --Chicago, Illinois
Skiing in Italy and a Chance Encounter, 1957... 141
Visiting Rome, 1957... 139
Visiting Central Indiana and Notre Dame, 1966... 148
  -- Indianapolis, Indiana: The Trip
  --Fortville, Indiana, and Geist Reservoir
  --Holy Cross at Notre Dame
  --Photos: 1966
    The 2000 Reunion: Holy Cross Class of 1955 (ND Class of 1960)... 161
  --The First Day
  --Friday Night, Before The Big Game
  --The Nebraska/Notre Dame Football Game
  --That Evening
--ACKNOWLEDGEMENTS... 169
--HOLY CROSS CLASS... 172
--NOTRE DAME: INDEX OF NAMES... 173

PREP SCHOOL DAYS (from the back cover...)

Older brother, Norm, emphasized, "At Holy Cross, there's no physical contact except on the playing fields." I surmised I'd have to give up fist fights, a survival occupation in our home town, the railroad, coal mining & steel mill city of Pittsburgh.

Speltz possessed a practiced skill at painting. I attempted to keep pace. Green locker paint flowed down the brush handle onto my hand, making the brush hard to hold. Speltz laughed and threw me a towel. "Make sure most of it gets on the lockers," he said. His confidence was disconcerting.

"Where's the furnace?" I asked. The steam man slipped on leather gloves and threw open two five-foot iron doors. The blast of heat was considerable. Algeo's face lit up, his freckles as bright as the fire in the furnace.

Father Simmons was a square dance director for the Holy Cross musical "Oklahoma." The practice sessions became hilarious. Some of us practiced in the recreation room, in the classrooms before classes, and on the basketball court before—and sometimes during--games.

Notre Dame college students walked from main campus up St. Mary's road to the women's college. The Holy Cross Junior and Senior playing fields bordered the road. Football players would stop to watch one of our games, or throw a few passes, or talk football with us.

Andrew Stevans as Sheriff Andrew Carnes, in the Holy Cross musical "Oklahoma"

Andrew Stevans grew up in Pittsburgh Pennsylvania. He has worked as a farm hand, a Navy non-com, an IBM engineer, an adult-ed teacher, and an HR manager. He now lives in Northern Virginia.

INTRODUCTION

THINGS YOU OUGHT TO KNOW

For some time I had hoped to find a way to "give back" to Holy Cross for an excellent education that went far beyond books. Special thanks must be extended to the Holy Cross teaching Priests and the Sisters of Notre Dame who offered unwavering kindness, caring and understanding to all of us young men. Daily, we students were exposed to individuals "Living the Faith," and demonstrating exactly what the term meant in both the Catholic and Notre Dame traditions.

There are two additional reasons behind the effort to write the Holy Cross memoires. The first and foremost is simply the realization that my generation of classmates, as well as our former resident faculty and friends, are diminishing in numbers. The individuals who lived through these times and who would get the most enjoyment from the memoires, frankly, are dying.

A second reason--a selfish one--is an attempt to re-experience my intellectual and spiritual growth during these formative years. Unfortunately, a great deal of mischief (maybe the word is "misadventure") was going on during that time and I'm fairly sure I've overly compensated, leaning more toward telling the misadventures than measuring the spiritual growth. Please forgive me.

I must admit that the stories often took on a will of their own. Let me refer you to a wonderfully gifted story teller, Philip Gulley, a "Hoosier" (Indianan) all of his life. He provides my excuse:

"I was once asked by a man if I wrote stories the way they happened or the way they should have happened. Both, I told him. While all these stories have their origins in fact, I have been known to add a little window dressing. There is

never a story anywhere that couldn't be made a little better with embellishment, so I don't apologize for that." Thank you, Philip Gulley.

I dedicate this book to all those Holy Cross folk from that era, and those mentioned herein. Without them there would be no Holy Cross stories. I apologize if I've missed some notables.

I dedicate it to my wife, Louise, whose patience during the many hours I spent on the computer makes her blessed and possibly a candidate for sainthood.

I dedicate it to Father Dean O'Donnell, CSC, a gifted Holy Cross English professor who encouraged me to write even after reading my essays.

I dedicate it to my classmates, particularly Jim Callahan, who urged me over many years to write the Holy Cross memoires, but also to Tom Hayes, Jim Keating and Jerry Wood who verified time and place, and offered advice during the writing effort.

The author

Gulley, Philip: *For Everything a Season*, Multnomah Publications

HOLY CROSS SEMINARY GROUNDS
University of Notre Dame

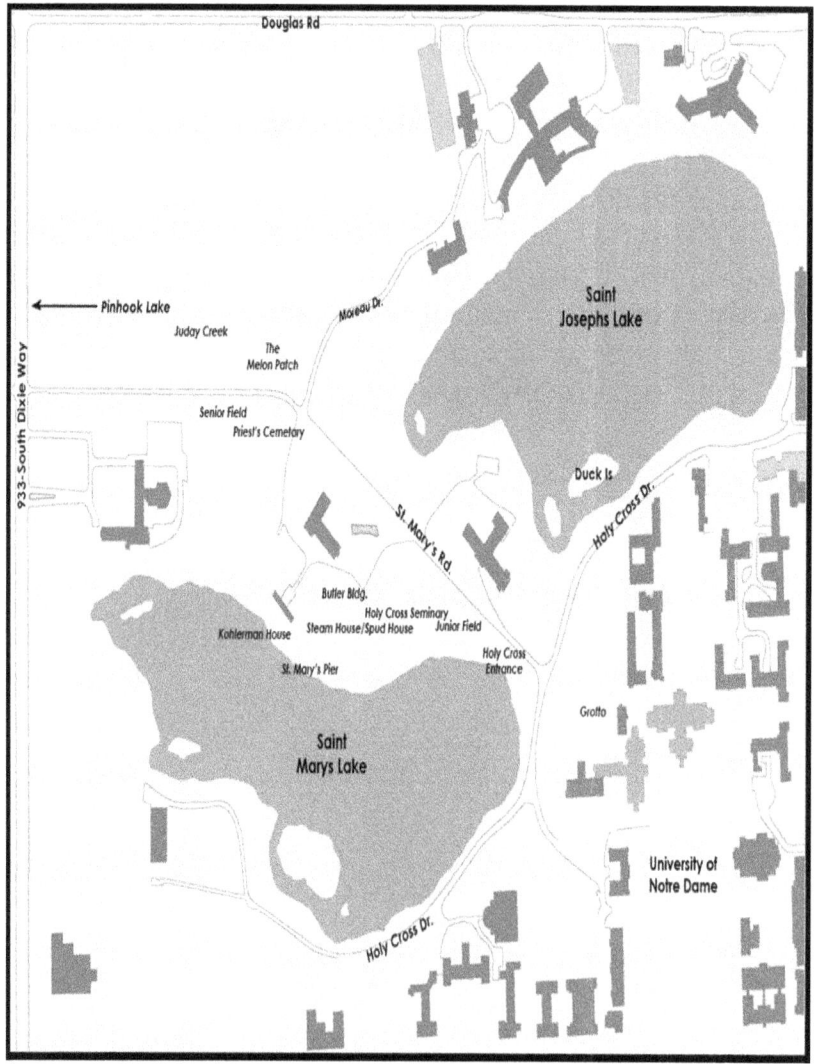

(courtesy of Michael Stevans)

...ARRIVAL...

PREP SCHOOL DAYS The Seminary at the University of Notre Dame

NOTRE DAME, INDIANA: HOLY CROSS

During the summer following a disastrous freshman year at St. James High School in West End, Pittsburgh, and the continued distractions of party going and close friends, I realized I was failing myself.

I had a religious side, Catholic beliefs gently pounded into me by the strict Sisters of Charity, during my elementary school years. I decided to join my closest sibling, Norm, and a few hundred others, at Holy Cross seminary, a preparatory school for the priesthood, housed in an imposing red-brick Victorian building, above St. Mary's lake, on the campus of the University of Notre Dame.

Older brothers Norm and Jack praised the daily regimen in a religious environment, noting the strong study discipline at Holy Cross and the strict daily routine*. Both brothers emphasized a "no bodily contact" rule (no horseplay) except on the playing field. It surprised me, at first, that they would mention this rule, and that I would have to give up fist fights, a survival occupation in our home town, the railroad, coal mining and steel mill city of Pittsburgh.

I thought back to sixth grade, following a lost summer recovering from rheumatic fever. I had struggled for two years to regain strength, performing daily push-ups, pull-ups, sit ups, running, and climbing up the sandstone cliffs near home.

Following seventh grade, my parents suggested I work the summer with older brother Jack's friend, on a farm an hour south of Pittsburgh, to continue regaining my strength. I jumped at the opportunity. Even then, I had read every "Country Gentleman" magazine I could lay my hands on. Farming was in the family's blood.

But, Holy Cross held other major attractions; the promise of year-round sports: organized teams for baseball, football, basketball—and there were pickup teams year round, including ice hockey on St. Mary's Lake when ice conditions permitted. Other interests became: muskrat trapping, fishing off a boat in St. Mary's lake, and doing lumbering on the property. During that sophomore year I was dubbed "Pierre, the lumberjack." Using a two-man saw, sledge hammers and metal wedges, Bill Klouda from Long Island and I spent weeks cutting large felled trees into manageable chunks for transport off the property.

And there was hiking, an interesting way to take a break from studies on a weekend and ply the waters of Juday creek, or swim across Pinhook Lake, located a short distance west of the Holy Cross senior playing field.

A week-day (school-day) schedule at Holy Cross… chapel at 6:50, breakfast at 7:30, daily assigned chore at 8:15, and classes from 8:45 until 11:30, Chapel (read religious books of student's choosing) until noon lunch, classes from 1:00 until 3:30 p.m., outside sports until 4:30. Cleanup and dinner at 5:15, recreation hall from 5:45 until 6:30, then study hall until 8:00, a break until 8:20, then Chapel and study hall again until 10:00. A "grand silence" (no talking) was expected from 10:00 p.m. until 7:30 breakfast the following day.

THE MELON PATCH

In mid-August I arrived at Holy Cross. Notre Dame and Holy Cross were not new to me. Since fifth grade I had been to Notre Dame twice a year with family to visit oldest brother, Jack, and later, my closest sibling, Norm. During the early spring of my freshman year at St. James, I had applied and was accepted at Holy Cross. Norm, a junior, and I traveled together on the New York Central train from Pittsburgh, Pennsylvania to South Bend, Indiana to begin an eventful fall term.

Juniors and seniors arrived a few weeks early to prepare Holy Cross for the incoming younger students. My sophomore classmates wouldn't arrive until early September.

Holy Cross housed up to 200 students, a dozen teaching priests and brothers, and several Sisters of Notre Dame who lived in their own quarters, a secure three-stories at the southwest corner of the house. Two of the nuns cooked for the entire house. A third nun ran the small dispensary and the house infirmary.

During this two week period, the daily 24-hour regimen, posted on the main corridor bulletin board, dictated bed at 10:00 p.m., arising at 6:30 a.m., chapel at 7:00, and breakfast at 8:00. The work day began at 9:00, and ended at

4:30. There were breaks for late morning chapel at 11:30, a hearty lunch at noon and at 4:30, cleanup, chapel and dinner at 6:00 p.m. The evening hours were spent casually in the recreation room reading, or playing board games, cards, or shooting pool or billiards until 9:00 p.m. chapel.

On that particularly bright, warm and cloudless afternoon, I sat on a section of the large lawn with Norm. Nearby was a statue of Mary, and further down the lawn was the St. Mary's Lake pier. An elm tree watched us from above, providing shade during the heat of the afternoon.

Norm challenged me to a game of mumblety peg. In Pittsburgh we called it mumbly peg. Norm and I shared my Boy Scout knife to play the game.

The objective of mumbly peg is to flip the knife into the ground from various positions on the body. The positions we used were the tips of all five fingers, the top of the hand, the elbow and finally the shoulder. Any miss by one player allowed the other to take over the play. Whoever stuck the knife into the ground first from the final shoulder position, won the game. Norm won easily almost pinning my foot with his shoulder flip. He got my attention.

Norm knew I had been suffering the pangs of homesickness, a nostalgia-like foreboding that began on my second day at Notre Dame. After Norm won mumbly peg, we walked north from Holy Cross, toward St. Mary's road. The half-mile long road ended at the women's college.

We passed the meticulously maintained priest cemetery where many Holy Cross priests were buried beneath ancient trees. The cemetery grounds were filled with upright concrete markers. I spotted a chipmunk. Norm remarked on the ever present chipmunk population. Chipmunks were always digging and nesting under the tombstones. Later in the fall, I would help classmates Jon Lullo from Chicago and Jerry Wood from Gary Indiana drown more than a few chipmunks out of their nests to save the tombstones from collapsing, truly God's work.

As we walked to the other side of the cemetery, Norm pointed out the senior athletic field on the left side of St. Mary's Road and Moreau Seminary baseball field to the right. Moreau housed senior seminarians who lived at Moreau and attended Notre Dame.

But something else had caught my eye: a large melon patch. I pointed out the ripe melons laying there for the taking. There had to be hundreds of them covering several acres. Norm looked at me with a bit of alarm. Stealing was not in his nature. On the other hand, I had a simple, straightforward philosophy. All the melons belonged to everyone in the world, but the two closest to the road belonged to Norm and me. This did not require deep thought. I was hungry. I grabbed the two melons.

Norm looked more apprehensive. "Well. I'm hungry too, but they've lain in the sun and may be too warm to eat. Besides, Brother Seraphim cared for them all summer. He won't be happy to see some missing." Norm was not convincing.

"There must be at least a thousand of them. Isn't St Mary's lake near by?" I asked.

Norm had his hands on his hips, and looking out over the melon patch, continued to make his decision.

"We can take one. That should do us 'till diner," he mumbled. He appeared somewhat relieved.

"I already cut through the stem on two of them. Let's take them both down to the lake."

Andrew Stevans

Norm grabbed one of the melons from my arms and quickly walked across the senior playing field into the woods. Through the trees I could see St. Mary's lake, glistening from the afternoon sun, beckoning us. As we walked, Norm pointed out a wild strawberry patch to avoid. He explained that, on visits, dad would walk around the lake to eat the wild strawberries in that patch. Having been raised on a farm, dad had an encyclopedic knowledge of eatable wild things. Here I was skirting his favorite strawberry patch hundreds of miles from home. I suddenly felt less homesick.

We deposited one of the melons in the shallow water under a large weeping willow. We then both climbed out on a large branch and sat facing each other, perched above the lake. I cut into the melon with the Boy Scout knife, and we devoured a king's meal of fresh, sweet melon, dropping any remains into the lake.

After a too short time and a long talk about bike hikes back home, Norm and I headed to the main grounds of Holy Cross. I felt at peace for the rest of the day. I'm not so sure about Norm's feelings, helping his younger brother steal melons in his first week at the seminary.

I returned to the lake the next day to eat the last melon, but couldn't find it. Maybe it had sunk into the lake mud, I thought, or, more likely, Norm had returned it to the melon patch. I retrieved another melon, and later, another. I may have experienced a few qualms of conscience, but they were quickly dispelled when the sophomore class arrived and most of the melons along St. Mary's Road disappeared. I still have the Boy Scout knife.

FISHING WITH DAVIS
THE TACKLE BOX

Thanks to seventh and eighth grade manual training once each week, back in Pittsburgh, older brother Norm and I learned shop skills early. We built our own fishing rods from scratch. First we bought a six-foot rod and several line-guides. We wrapped each line guide with wire, evenly spaced along the rod's surface and soldered each one. The final line-guide was a special end guide soldered at the far end of the rod. We also bought and soldered a cork wrapped handle onto the other end of the rod to hold our precious reels. We didn't take our fishing gear to Holy Cross, and though I did little fishing at home, I missed my fishing equipment.

I soon developed a friendship with a Notre Dame, Old College student, Tom Davis. Davis had an enviable collection of home-made fishing flies. He enjoyed trying out his new creations and offered to teach me his skills.

"You don't want to scare the fish away. Throw the fly with an easy swing of the rod, and let the fly land the way it's supposed to, like a bug on the water." I took Davis's fishing rod and copied his style of casting from a boat. Over a period of two weeks, we spent several hours in the middle of St. Mary's Lake doing his brand of fly fishing with a short rod.

During these wonderful days, the late August sun seemed cooler than usual, our wide brimmed hats deflecting much of the direct sunlight. Often, a breeze found its way across St. Mary's providing us and the aluminum boat a small nudge toward the Holy Cross shore line.

"I prefer lures to fly fishing," I finally explained to Tom. Back then the "Jitterbug" was the lure of choice and I had brought mine. Davis agreed to loan me a rod and reel, and the following day he brought along his tackle box. The tackle box opened with double drawers expanding on either side. It contained a deep bottom for larger items. Davis had another reel stored in there. To my young eyes there was a prince's ransom worth of fishing lures and flies, catgut, spools of nylon fishing line, lead sinkers, plastic floats and every imaginable fisherman's resource for weighing, measuring and cleaning fish. Everything in the tackle box appeared neatly arranged. In recent years, I've been distracted from fishing. Yet, to this day I haven't seen a tackle box better organized or more complete than Davis's.

For the remaining few days before the freshmen and sophomore's arrival, Tom continued fly fishing and caught two small mouth bass. I continued with my Jitterbug fishing, finally switching to night crawlers and caught a few sunfish.

Fr. Corcoran, in his prized wooden boat, holding a freshly caught, 14 inch small-mouth bass: St. Mary's Lake, 1953

KOHLERMAN HOUSE

One major effort undertaken by a fellow seminarian was to build a large aluminum shed on a concrete pad--from scratch. Father Chuck Kohlerman, CSC, back then a senior in my brother, Norm's class, was a devoted carpenter and a one-man act. Kohlerman decided to build the large structure himself—or, with volunteers, if anyone would offer to help. The structure, Norm recalls, was 120 feet long. It set near St. Mary's Lake, about 100 yards southwest of the steam house.

Earlier that summer, while at home in Pittsburgh, Norm and I had helped two contracted carpenters build a bedroom, bathroom and kitchen eating area onto the first floor of our parent's home. Later, that same summer, I was a new arrival at Holy Cross, and in my sophomore year. Norm and I decided to help Mr. Kohlerman complete "Kohlerman House."

Surprisingly, Kohlerman already had poured the concrete pad and built a skeleton framework. We undertook enclosing the sides with corrugated metal sheeting. We attached the overlapping three foot by eight foot sheets with galvanized, three-inch cotter pins.

We fed each cotter pin through Kohlerman's earlier pre-drilled holes, then twisted the cotter pin on the inside of the shed with a pair of pliers. It's hard to imagine affixing just a hundred of the cotter pins--while holding and lining-up each sheet. Every few feet we had to push the cotter pins through not only two layers of overlapped, corrugated sheeting, but also through the frame of the shed, making it an even more tedious operation. It seemed like Norm and I approached the thousand cotter pin mark by the time the outside walls were completed.

We began enclosing the roof. We followed a similar procedure to the siding and, to this day, I don't recall how we kept the roof from leaking through the pre-drilled, cotter-pinned holes, onto the concrete below. Other than for the heat of the direct sun, covering the roof was no more tedious an operation than the siding. Of course there was always the possibility of falling through to the concrete, below. This was definitely young men's work.

After hearing that my brother, Norm, and I had helped build Kohlerman House, several classmates asked what the large structure was used for.

"It's a garage, storage unit and workshop," I would respond. I viewed the structure with a great pride of accomplishment.

Later, Tom Hayes confirmed my description, "A few years after our graduation from Holy Cross, Brother Christopher Bowers used the shed as a fully equipped workshop, providing new Holy Cross brothers technical training."

Hayes then went on to describe the training and the fact that one of our classmates, (Brother) Duane Boudreaux, CSC, from Oklahoma, was taught shop skills by Brother Bowers, at Kohlerman House.

Hayes should know all about fully equipped machine shops. For many years he was a master tool and die maker, and most likely knows more than a thing or two about what Brother Bowers taught. Hayes described the still standing structure as an eye-sore. "Always was," he emphasized.

PAINTING LOCKERS WITH DE LAWD

Norm introduced me to some of the upper classmen. Norm knew I had worked a few summers painting ours or a neighbor's home, so I was teamed up with Cy Speltz, an Iowa native, to do some locker painting in the freshman and sophomore locker rooms, located in the large, brightly lit basement of Holy Cross. There had to be a hundred full sized lockers in all.

Speltz appeared to be in great physical condition and sported a dark tan. He had a laid-back, friendly, engaging way about him. He also possessed a practiced skill at painting quickly and efficiently. I struggled to keep up with him. In my haste green locker paint flowed down the brush handle onto my hand, making the brush slippery to hold. Speltz laughed when he saw the problem and threw me a towel.

"Make sure most of it gets on the lockers," he said. He returned to his fast pace. In a matter of a few hours we had painted a few dozen lockers. My contribution totaled several.

Some time later, Norm showed up to see how we were doing—maybe to see how I was doing--addressing Speltz as "De Lawd."

"How're De Lawd and my brother doing?" he said laughing with Speltz. Speltz explained that Norm had been calling him "De Lawd" since they had attended a movie the previous year. The movie, "The Green Pastures" was Old Testament stories retold from an early American, black perspective.

"Now, you get on outta here devil, or I'll drill you with muh 45," Speltz replied in a deep, bass voice, never missing a stroke with his brush.

Norm walked off. "Brother, you'd better do De Lawd's work carefully, or there'll be HELL to pay!"

Speltz continued to chuckle to himself. "That brother of yours is a good example for us evil doers," he said. "You can't go wrong with a brother like Norm."

After a short time, Speltz opened up, talking about his camping days and his love of the outdoors, hunting and fishing. He said he'd like to feed the entire house on the fish he caught from St. Mary's lake. For several weeks during the late summer and fall of the following year, Speltz floated multiple baited hooks spread across the lake and actually fed the junior and senior classes with St. Mary's lake fish, small mouth bass and sunfish, he had caught and frozen.

Speltz also had an interest in muskrat trapping. He said the pelts were valuable, and he promised to show me how to trap, skin and dry a muskrat pelt in order to get top price. The money, he explained, went into a pool of funds for the Holy Cross foreign missions.

We painted on. Speltz described a major painting project he wanted to accomplish before leaving Holy Cross: repainting the Christmas statuary that made up the manger scene at Sacred Heart Church, on main campus, something Speltz managed to accomplish before graduating from Holy Cross.

He was definitely a man of his word, and over time I found that "you couldn't go wrong with a friend like De Lawd."

During that first week, I enjoyed Speltz's ramblings. I'd ask him questions to keep him distracted from his painting, while continuing to paint lockers as fast as I could, hoping to catch up. I never did.

(Courtesy of Jerry Wood, Photo by Jim Keating)
Cy Speltz strumming away in the locker room, 1953

Making and Unmaking Beds... Speltz and I, along with a few dozen other students shared a dorm in one wing of the second floor of Holy Cross. Speltz was one of the dorm monitors, selected to maintain order and the rule of silence in the dorm.

Each morning beds had to be made. Following morning Mass, we would return to our dorms on the second or third floor of the building. There were no "fitted" sheets back then. Each bed required two sheets of twin size, tucked in, and a wool blanket spread over the top sheet. A second wool blanket was folded across the bottom of the bed. The pillow in its pillow case was left exposed. Each student placed a small, wooden crucifix on the pillow case.

When retiring for the night, Speltz took the loose top sheet and blanket and wrapped himself in it like a cocoon.

"Why do you wrap yourself up so you can't move under the sheets?" I finally asked.

Cy explained that he was used to sleeping outdoors in a sleeping bag. It was a more familiar way for him to get comfortable. He went on to explain the family's hardware store in Iowa, and his access to every possible outdoor item. He said it's where he bought his first muskrat traps. He promised to show me the traps.

Catching Muskrats... It was a few weeks into the fall months when Speltz and I met at the spud room atop the steam house. He took several traps that were hanging on the wall, and we walked down by the lake.

I'll show you my technique for catching muskrat, and, after we catch one, I'll show you how to skin and dry the pelt to get top price for it, for the missions.

"When you set the trap, place it underwater, near where the muskrat enters and leaves his nest. Sooner or later he's going to brush by the trap and we've got him." I was instructed to avoid any direct contact with the set trap for up to a week, yet checking it daily from land or by boat and as silently as possible. We caught many muskrats. Many of the pelts that I cleaned became stiff or were not skinned properly for selling. With his honed skill, Cy usually ended up skinning and drying them.

Photographing the Swans; Lake Debris... We knew that trash was occasionally found in St. Mary's Lake.

Throwing any kind of waste in either St. Joe's or St. Mary's was a serious infraction of campus rules.

On a cool weekend in the late fall, Speltz and I were out in one of the aluminum boats, near the Rockne Hall end of St. Mary's Lake, trying to photograph two white swans in a formation: either swimming together, or facing each other. It was late in the day, and we couldn't get the swans to cooperate. While we waited patiently, we noticed several Notre Dame men, walking quickly around the lake, stop momentarily and throw empty cans into the lake near the Holy Cross pier. We both yelled to them, only to get a wave back. By the time we had rowed across the lake to the pier, the men had disappeared. Over the next several days, we waited at the back steam room door, with a full view of the pier, trying to catch anyone repeating their behavior, but were not successful.

We were concerned that anyone swimming off the pier could step on a can or a broken bottle. We then realized that the bottom of the lake around the Holy Cross pier area would have to be cleaned of all debris the following spring.

Cy Speltz photographing Swans on St. Mary's Lake

Andrew Stevans

MORTIER: MONITOR, LINEMAN

I had finished the first week at Holy Cross. My homesickness had diminished. My old attitude partially returned, and I assumed some Pittsburgh hooligan characteristics that I was determined to shake.

Speltz and I had painted our way completely through the sophomore locker room and had begun painting in the junior locker room at the south end of the basement, nearer St. Mary's lake. Speltz and I had adapted to each others painting quirks. Actually, thinking back, Speltz had adapted to my painting quirks. Over several days he suggested a better way to hold my brush to acquire a more even stroke.

During the sophomore locker painting the previous week, my grey painter's drop cloth had taken on a more and more prominent green. Speltz explained how to use the side of the brush to paint inside the doors to limit dripping. I became frustrated with my inability to maintain Speltz's pace, but reconciled myself with the thought that I had gained efficiency and definitely some economy on the use of paint, thanks to Speltz's kind suggestions.

Following lunch, I returned to the locker room. My approach was suddenly blocked by a large junior who introduced himself as Mr. Mortier, a newly appointed sophomore monitor. I had seen him around Holy Cross.

In order to exert his authority, Mortier barked a few orders that I immediately ignored and told him in Pittsburgh slang to get out of my way. Thankfully, Mortier said nothing and walked ahead of me through the junior locker room. I followed, taunting him, urging him to throw a punch. I found out later from classmates that, aside from a puffy exterior--he outweighed me by at least 50 pounds--and a streak of arrogance, he excelled at sports.

Since bodily contact was forbidden except on the playing fields, any fist fight might well have ended both of our stays at Holy Cross. But I was the only sophomore there at the time, so, for his own reasons, Mortier, whom I had never seen smile, felt obligated to rattle my chain. I became wary of him from that day on.

During the fall of the following year, I had gained some weight at 185 pounds, and played halfback positions in football. To this day I don't know how I ended up as a lineman facing off with Maurie Mortier. During that one-year's time, Mortier's pudginess had streamlined itself to a solid 250 pounds or more. I was a strong blocker for my size, and proud of my ability to maneuver quickly. I also knew how to hit an opponent as low as possible, pushing forward and up, knocking him off balance before he was aware of my speed.

I hit Mortier low, fast and hard. Before he knew what had happened he fell backwards, landing hard on the ground. I smiled and returned to the huddle. Without paying the least attention to me, Mortier got up off the ground and lined up for the next play.

The ball was centered. I hit the ground. Mortier had waited for the split second when I was at my lowest approach, and coming up. He hit me square across the chest, lifting me up and pushing me backwards. It was fast and effective. I was dazed when Mortier reached forward to help me up. He smiled. I should have stuck to halfback.

Tower Hill, Warren Dunes State Park, Michigan, 1952

THE TOWER HILL INCIDENT

As a thanks for the juniors and seniors hard work cleaning up the house for soon to arrive freshmen and sophomores, one morning in late August we all crowded onto a bus and began an hour or so trip to Dunes State Park—The Dunes--on the southeastern shore of Lake Michigan. The trip would include enjoying some great company among the group, an anticipated race to the top of the highest dune, Tower Hill, swimming in the chilly waters of Lake Michigan and a lot of good food, set up later near the bus parking area.

The group told jokes and voiced their frustration over Michigan State's win against Notre Dame in previous seasons. Since the bus passed by Niles, Michigan, just over the State border from Indiana—and, in our opinion, deep into Michigan territory--the chant began: "We don't give a damn for the whole State of Michigan, we're from Notre Dame."

Our Notre Dame group thoroughly nailed the Niles residents with the chant—I recall several kids riding bikes, some elderly folk walking down a sidewalk, and a bum crossing the train tracks. Not to be silenced, we sang "row, row, row your boat," and "pauper sum ego" in three part harmony.

"Pauper sum ego (I am poor)
Nihil Habeo (I have nothing)
Et nihil dabo" (and I'll give nothing)

The Latin "Pauper Sum Ego" sung in harmony by strong men's voices, filled the bus and echoed down the quiet, late morning streets. I wondered if my sophomore class had a choral group.

Some miles before arriving at the lake, I could see Lake Michigan rising up above the horizon. I felt somewhat disoriented and a bit on edge seeing for the first time an immense body of water that appeared poised above us. Everyone else on the bus took it in stride.

As we entered the park, Norm came from the back of the bus and cautioned me about the race to the top of Tower Hill. Each runner in the group was determined to reach the top before anyone else. I was anxious to experience the competitiveness within the group. Norm had been unbeaten since his sophomore year. That morning at breakfast, he had heard through friends that the juniors had planned a delaying action.

"Stay with me because I get the feeling the juniors want Doyle to win."

I found out later that Doyle's vanguard consisted of a small group of juniors mostly from the Chicago area. Seminary rules didn't allow cliques. I realized I wasn't alone in my inclination to break house rules.

From the entrance to the Dunes State Park, the bus followed a dirt road that ended at a large, circular parking area. The bus began a wide turn, following the wooden stanchions around the lot. After situating itself facing out of the park, it rolled to a stop. Everyone stood at once. A surge of bodies began pushing toward the bus exits.

Several of the juniors were attempting to block Norm's exit while several others jumped off the bus and ran toward a wooded path leading to the dunes. Norm and I both hit the blockade with our shoulders and ducked under a few arms, easily reaching the bus doors. On the beginning trail others were awaiting Norm. A struggle began as several juniors tried to grab Norm and hold onto him. I threw a few punches at one of the juniors; I think it was Houk, a Hoosier. He ducked. Norm threw a block at one guy and I swung hard at another as the path cleared. We continued at a fast run.

In short sprints I could beat Norm, but I couldn't match his aggressive stride for long. We slowly caught up to Doyle and two others who began serpentining back and forth across the road, allowing Doyle to stay ahead. Norm took off with a burst of speed and I followed. Already out of breath, I spotted Tower Hill down the macadam road, a huge sand hill created over many millennia by the heavy beating winds from the Chicago side of the lake, 100 miles to the west. I gained a respect for Chicago's nickname "the windy city" when I later noticed how far the dune had separated itself from the shore line of the lake.

Tower Hill rose up a hundred yards or more on a steep, 45 degree grade. Norm yelled encouragement, as he advanced up the hill ahead of me.

"You'll get your second wind, just keep running."

I approached the base of the dune and began climbing. After each stride I felt my foot slip back in the sand a half stride. I wasn't getting my second breath as Norm had promised. Many yards ahead of me, Norm kept up his pace.

"Keep moving, don't stop, and when you get to the top, keep walking or you'll get leg cramps." I felt some desperation.

My body moved upward, my legs churning in the sand. I couldn't gulp sufficient air and began gasping for more when I experienced a change to my labored breathing. I breathed with less desperation and yet continued to expend the same amount of effort. Doyle passed me. I slowly, painfully reached the top.

Doyle shook Norm's hand, acknowledging his victory. They shared some comments and both laughed. Doyle approached me as his two partners arrived. We all continued gasping for breath. I had leaned forward, my hands on my knees. Doyle said, "Keep moving; don't let yourself relax or you'll cramp up." I smiled to exhibit some bravado. I wanted to collapse to the ground and lay on my back, but coaches Norm and Doyle knew what they were talking about. After several minutes of forced walking, I glanced out at Lake Michigan marveling at its immensity. Slowly, I returned to normal. My breathing had slowed, and my legs were losing their tightness. I faked a calm demeanor for the newly arriving runners.

Norm had already started his descent to the bottom of Tower Hill. I took long strides, running and sinking, a completely new sensation, almost falling downhill to catch up. We both changed into our swim suits and walked to the beach. The water was bitter cold at first. We both enjoyed swimming, so plunged into waves that were determined to push us back to shore. After a too short period of swimming and walking the beach with friends, we returned to the bus to assist in setting up for lunch. Nothing more was said about the Tower Hill incident.

It would be my first and most exciting of several trips to "The Dunes," over the next three years.

Tower Hill, Warren Dunes State Park, Michigan, 1954

Rog Sowala, Charley Chavez, Jim Glaza (Courtesy: Jerry Wood, Photo: Jim Keating)
**Tom Norris, Jon Lullo, Dick Cadieux,
Carl Bufalini, & Ed Hines**

...SOPHOMORE YEAR...

MEETING CLASSMATES

    Another sunny early September Northern Indiana day had dawned when freshmen and sophomores began arriving at the locker rooms of Holy Cross. A number of students in my class introduced themselves. Jim Glaza and Jim Keating, both from Michigan, had cameras and film they'd brought from home. I began to relax and discussed my interest in photography. I mentioned that a school friend in Pittsburgh had won photography awards in elementary school. His father, A. Martin Hermann, was a prize winning photographer for the Pittsburgh Press, our home newspaper.
    Norm Lakatos, from Ohio, had a locker near mine. Norm reminded me of a cousin I'd grown up with. In later years, this cousin and I would join the Navy together.
    I remember Jon Lullo, Tom Norris, both from Chicago, and Jerry Wood, from Gary Indiana, arguing quietly about something having to do with sports.
    I had met Tom Hayes brother, John, earlier. Even in the heat of mid-summer, John ran St. Joe's Lake almost daily. I don't remember personally meeting Tom Hayes that day, but I

heard him blaring out some news in his deep bass, as he walked across the locker room. I wondered who he was. Over the coming months and years I'd get used to Tom's friendly, blustery, matter-of-fact voice. Tom reminded me of a young Friar Tuck, from the movie "Robin Hood."

It amazed me, and provided some comfort, that my classmates would break a locker room silence rule on their first day back to Holy Cross. Several remained to say where they were from and discussed among themselves the fall school schedule. They also discussed a few former students who were not returning due to failing grades or mischief making.

I felt at home with this pleasant group, and promised myself to turn over a new leaf, hit the books hard, and hide my aggressive nature, keeping it in check for the football field.

VISITING FATHER FIEDLER

If you can imagine a strong, disciplined, no-nonsense, unpretentious man, who often hid his kind and caring side, you're most likely thinking of Father Joseph "Harry" Fiedler. It wasn't long after my sophomore classmates arrived at Holy Cross that I was summoned by Father Fiedler. I had already heard about Father Fiedler's interest in sports, his natural athletic ability, and the rumor of an earlier association with a Chicago White Sox farm team.

I also knew Father Fiedler had a hearing problem and allowed myself to be entertained by students describing the results of whispering in Latin class to answer Father's question. When Father adjusted his hearing aid volume the student would talk normally causing Father to quickly turn down the volume. I also knew that Father Fiedler was the director of studies at Holy Cross.

As I entered the room, Father was right to the point, "Mr. Stevans, you'll have to select a priest as a spiritual advisor as soon as possible. Also, I want you to retake first year Latin."

"Yes Father. Well, would you be my spiritual advisor?" It was a spontaneous request, since I'd come unprepared.

"Of course I will. Thanks for stopping by."

That was it. I left the room and continued down to the sophomore locker room to find out what a spiritual advisor was, and what I had just committed to. There were several classmates in the locker room. We were supposed to follow a silence rule while there. I motioned to Callahan. Callahan was from Youngstown, a sister city to my hometown of Pittsburgh. Like my other new classmates, he was a reliable source of information on the workings of Holy Cross. Callahan always had a welcoming demeanor; a smiling, cordial way about him.

"What is a priest spiritual advisor?" I whispered.

"We have to select one each year. Don't worry about it. It's a good thing," Callahan whispered back. Then with his ever present smile, Callahan disappeared down the hallway to attend mandatory chapel before dinner. I followed, not sure of what I had just been told.

Later, during evening recreation, I brought up the question again. This time it was directed at Cavanaugh, another Youngstown native. I could hear a far off symphony playing, as he removed his headphones.

"Everyone's required to have a spiritual advisor. Spiritual advisors keep you out of trouble." I thought I noticed his eyes narrow a bit, and searched for sarcasm in his voice.

Cavanaugh replaced his headphones, and turned back to his symphony. I didn't pursue the matter further. I added Cavanaugh to my "not so sure about" list.

Later that year, Father Fiedler assigned Cavanaugh the responsibility of house librarian. On trips to the library I would find Cavanaugh a font of knowledge. He was not overflowing with warmth, but was definitely an OK guy.

For example, all students had permission to read religious books in chapel before lunch. Father Riley monitored this activity. Several times I asked Cavanaugh to suggest a book. Some of his recommendations were "The Silver Chalice", "The Robe" and "Modern Miracles." Cavanaugh didn't raise an eyebrow when I later checked out "The Scarlet Letter, "Gone With The Wind," and several of the Hardy Boys series. Of course he assumed I'd read these out of chapel.

I soon decided that I couldn't go wrong with Father Fiedler as my spiritual advisor since he was a supportive director of studies. Even though he came across as a no nonsense kind of guy, I tried on several occasions to engage Father in conversations. I once asked why he had a large trunk at the foot of his bed. It was obviously meticulously maintained, shiny black with ornamental hinges and a sophisticated metal design across the top. It appeared to be his sole possession. The rest of his room was Spartan, containing a small bed, a lighted desk, and a closet on the far side of the room. The floor had no rug.

I had hoped for an entertaining anecdote, perhaps one about the trunk traveling across Europe with an aunt who presented it to him years earlier. This had actually happened to my oldest brother, Jack, who inherited his trunk from a great aunt.

Father was dismissive about it, but quick to comment that soon I would be asked to take a vow of poverty as he had. He launched into a short lecture on the priesthood and poverty. I was afraid to ask what he had in the closet.

For me, geometry would be that year's nemesis. It came to pass, as the sophomore year flew by, that I'd often find myself with a frustrating, unsolvable geometry problem. The problem seemed to have little supportive proof from the list of axioms and corollaries that made up geometry. I would reluctantly join the line of other frustrated students at Father Fiedler's door, seeking his learned advice. He never failed me.

In pick-up games of two-hand-touch football, or on the basketball court, Father Fiedler would often join in. He was in his early 50's and a large man, but agile for his size. His hands were immense and I imagined him pounding in fence posts on the family farm, or catching a line drive without effort. His hands had obviously done heavy labor.

Lee Skinner, a classmate and friend from Chicago, and an avid hand ball player, mentioned Father Fiedler's skill on the handball court. With apparent ease he could move and change direction quickly, and often won.

It appeared he enjoyed many sports, and could easily compete against much younger men on the playing field, and on the basketball and handball courts.

In 1966 I revisited Holy Cross with my wife, baby daughter, and 4-year old son. I had hoped to visit with a few of my newly ordained Holy Cross classmates, Fathers Sowala, Whelan, and Kaiser. I understood all three were at Notre Dame at the time.

It was Father Fiedler who met and entertained us in grand style for several hours, along with Father Pete Sandonato. Father Fiedler attempted more than once to phone

PREP SCHOOL DAYS The Seminary at the University of Notre Dame

Sowala, my former quarter-back over 10 years earlier. Sowala was on the golf course and couldn't be reached.

All too soon, the priests had to leave for chapel. I asked for Father Fiedler's blessing. He blessed the family, smiled and shook my hand. That meeting would be our last.

FOUR-PART, A CAPPELLA CHOIR

One evening in the fall a few of us sophomores were talking casually in the recreation (rec) room. We had been listening to a Mario Lanza recording that Dick Cavanaugh brought from his home in Ohio. The subject of a sophomore 4-part choir came up. Lee Skinner and Harry Krush, both Chicagoans with considerable piano skills, offered to take turns directing the choir, if a 4-part choir could be assembled. We decided to pass the word among our classmates. We would meet the following evening in one of the upstairs classrooms.

Twelve showed up, an impressive figure in Skinners estimation. We sang several songs together. It became immediately obvious that Dick Cavanaugh, Jon Lullo and Tom Hayes would sing bass. Mike Gelven, Joe Schott, Cy Speltz and I were designated first tenors; Jim Callahan, Jim Keating, Lee Skinner and Jerry Wood second tenors; and Jim Glaza, Harry Krush and Ron Vogel baritones.

Under Skinner's direction, we began learning the harmony of a 4-part "*O Esca Viatorum.*" Krush, witty and sarcastic, complained that the acoustics of the room were so poor the 4-part would sound more like 12 voices in a shower. We moved the meeting to the library.

Krush, like Skinner, a superb pianist, could easily read music and taught the baritones and basses their parts. Skinner picked out the melody and harmony on the piano, and instructed each of the four groups. We picked up our parts quickly.

In surprisingly short order, the 4-part a cappella group was ready to sing together. The sound was a perfect blend of voices. As we ended the "O Esca Viatorum," we heard the echo of our voices in the hallway, then silence. Even Krush, not one to be easily pleased, seemed surprised and fascinated by the product of a 30 minute effort.

The following Sunday happened to be Visitors Sunday, when parents visited the students at Holy Cross. Our a cappella group requested that we sing the High Mass with the senior 2-part choir. Naturally, we offered to sing the 4-part "O Esca Viatorum," during Communion.

At 9:00 a.m., the chapel slowly filled with students, many with their families. We 12 sophomores joined the seniors in the choir loft to sing the High Mass. The senior choir sang a 2-part Kyrie with organ accompaniment, followed by Father Harold Riley, our Superior, giving a short sermon, and thanking the visiting parents for coming.

The Mass Communion began with the choirs singing the Pater Noster (Our Father). A few of the parents joined in. Father Riley began "Domine, non sum dignus..." (Lord, I am not worthy...). Skinner raised his hand for our attention and from a small, round, pitch-pipe he sounded the notes for each of the four groups.

As communicants approached the alter, we began in perfect unison, following Skinner's direction. The a cappella voices rose and fell in harmony, "*O Esca Viatorum, Panis Angelorum...*"

Following the final stanza, a complete silence fell over the chapel. Not until Father Riley began voicing the final Mass prayers did we notice the shaking in his voice. It became the first of many 4-part Masses for our a cappella group.

Frequently, for the resident Holy Cross priests celebrating daily Mass away from the chapel, a few of us would sing their Mass in Gregorian chant, choosing one of the psalms to plan how we would sing the Introit, Gradual, Offertory and Communion verses. We became so adept at applying a psalm to a Mass that we could plan the psalm, marking the ups and downs of the psalm chosen, a few minutes before a Mass.

On the passing of a Notre Dame priest, the choir sang the Mass for the Dead at Sacred Heart Church on the Notre Dame campus. All Holy Cross students attended these Masses. Following Mass, the death knell tolled and we joined the procession for the half-mile walk to the Priest's Cemetery, behind Holy Cross.

Over the months the unique sound of a dozen young men singing Latin Mass music and Christmas hymns in 4-part a cappella, came to the attention of Father Bill McAuliffe, the Notre Dame and Holy Cross choir director. By our junior year we had gained some local fame. A Christmas bus tour was arranged and the choir sang at St. Joe Hospital and several retirement homes in and around South Bend, Indiana.

Courtesy of Mary Lou Klouda
Bill Klouda

LATIN & LUMBERJACKS

Bill Klouda, a sophomore from Long Island, was extremely bright and well respected for it. He towered over many of his classmates. He became a close friend and fellow confidant.

Klouda was a year ahead of me in Latin and occasionally wrote out Latin translations when I ran into problems. I recall his long-hand was like script from a typewriter, not at all like my scribble.

Several of us self-proclaimed athletes would discuss conditioning exercises, the objective to increase our upper and lower body strength without using weights. Klouda listened to these discussions quietly. Like me he considered daily conditioning exercises against the rules.

Spindly, with long legs and thin arms, Klouda appeared weak, but we knew he had strength. He batted as a lefty, and when he connected with the ball, it typically flew into the far right field, or became a solid line-drive through the in-field.

During the late fall, Father Fiedler, director of studies and also in charge of the Holy Cross grounds, asked if I'd like to cut up some large, felled trees lying near the junior playing field.

"I need to get those trees cut into manageable sizes to load in a truck and haul off the property. I have some heavy-duty wedges, a couple of sledgehammers and a two-man saw. Are you interested?" Father already knew I'd be receptive to any kind of physical activity, but I had to find someone as interested as I was to be my other half on the two-man saw. Klouda might be interested, I thought. He seemed anxious to build up his too tall somewhat thin physique.

"Yes, Father, and I think Klouda might be interested too. I'll check with him. When do you want us to start?"

"Could you get started tomorrow, after your football game? Remember, this is a commitment of at least several weeks, and there are other trees that I can have felled. You can cut those up as well."

"Father, they're fairly large trees."

"Yes, they average 3 to 4 feet across. That's why you'll need a two-man saw." Father said. I became excited about lumbering more than I let on. I knew Klouda would be as well.

The next day, after our two-hand touch football games, Klouda and I met Father Fiedler at the steam house.

"Make sure to store the tools back in the steam house."

"Yes Father. Thank you."

Klouda and I looked at each other with un-erasable smiles. What a racket we had fallen into. We would emerge fit as lumberjacks and have some enjoyment while doing it.

I became so dedicated to the tree-cutting job that my football team's quarterback, Sowala, began calling me "Pierre." The nickname stuck.

Both Klouda and I adapted quickly to the two-man saw routine, but were surprised how much of an effort it became to saw through a yard of solid oak. After the saw cut into the wood and sunk an additional several inches, we tried tapping a steel wedge into the cut to open and spread the log. Sawing then became much easier. We sawed and tapped, sawed and tapped until the log fell into two pieces. We completed the process, sawing through the logs, until we had many sections of tree trunk, each section several feet long. We then split each section of log into four pieces. To complete one tree trunk took a week and a half, working an hour each day. Then we began sawing up another trunk, and another.

Father Fiedler decided not to fell other trees. Klouda and I conspired to use the time each day to exercise, but we needed a place to work out. In short order we discovered the "cave", the movie auditorium beneath the refectory. At the far end of the auditorium a stage had been constructed some years earlier. Behind the stage a room had been built that was ideal for working out.

We developed a work-out routine. On alternate days, in mid-afternoon, we did 30 minutes of either upper or lower body exercises beneath the refectory. Part of our regimen required that we gain weight. Following dinner, we visited the refectory, walking over to the waiters table for conversation and a few extra glasses of milk to pack on the pounds.

Andrew Stevans

I recall one day when Klouda surprised me, asking me for help with a Latin translation. Father Banas presented his Latin class with the following phrase: *Toti emul esto*. The class was provided a clue. The inscription appeared on an ancient post in the middle of a town. Father promised extra credit for anyone who could explain what it said.

That evening, Klouda seemed up tight, and asked me for any help to translate the phrase. My helping Klouda with a Latin translation was almost laughable. But he looked sincere, so I spent study time that evening trying to help my friend. At the end of study hall, Klouda came over to my desk, asking if I had come up with a translation. I said "I think it translates *He's full of emul,* whatever *emul* is. I can't find a translation for *emul..*" Klouda snickered to himself as he sometimes did, and left for evening chapel.

The next day Klouda reported that he had passed my translation around class, anonymously, before Father Banas arrived. He then explained Father Banas's answer to the puzzling phrase.

"Father wrote on the board, "*Toti emul esto = To tie mules to.*"

"What!" I'm sure I became quiet for a moment, probably amused that Klouda had passed around my translation, but mad at myself for wasting so much vital study time on such a simple problem. The writing on the ancient post was in English. It wasn't Latin at all.

THE RACE AROUND ST. JOE'S LAKE

When sports are mandatory, sooner or later winning on the playing field becomes an ingrained, subconscious desire to win at everything. And everyone becomes a competitor. Even in the final days of winter, we played outdoor sports, including ice-hockey on St. Mary's lake, football on either the junior or senior playing fields, and, at the beginning of spring, baseball team assignments, a sport that would take us into June and then home for our summer vacations.

Although Father Larry LeVasseur can't be held directly responsible for the elimination races around St Joe Lake, his dare to race Henry Reyes, a speedy Texas Long-Horn fan, in front of the entire Holy Cross student body, set off a chain reaction of sorts. Racing became a minor obsession over the next several weeks.

Larry Mulkerin, a Pittsburgher, taller than me and large chested, was an endurance runner according to the few who ran against him and lost. I considered myself to be fast; a strong runner for about a half-mile--if I paced myself. I decided, after an earlier Tower Hill race, I'd leave long-distance running to my older brother, Norm.

The question was raised following a touch football game on the junior field.

"Did you hear Mulkerin is challenging anyone to beat him in a race around St. Joe Lake?"

Word spread quickly.

Until recently, I had been running St Mary's lake several times a week to maintain my stamina. I still hadn't caught up in my studies from the bad freshman year at St. James, in Pittsburgh. There were soon-to-be mid-semester tests. I had to cram for them. But I was interested in Mulkerin's challenge.

No one had seen Mulkerin practice running St. Joe's lake. I recall it was Coyne from Michigan who confided this lack of conditioning detail to me. I broke a divisional silence rule, and asked Tom Hayes older brother, John, a senior and a frequent runner of St Joe Lake, if he had observed Mulkerin running. He hadn't.

I didn't challenge Mulkerin right away. I played daily team sports, but kept my work outs and runs around St. Mary's lake to a minimum during the heavy study period.

The rains and warm breezes of an early spring were welcome in northern Indiana. By early March the lakes had thawed, and someone had announced that small-mouth bass were spawning near the edge of St Mary's lake. Speltz and I, and several others had to have a look. In the process we discovered several other small-mouth bass hovering over their eggs along the lake shallows. My focus on lake activities brought to mind the Mulkerin challenge.

I approached him in front of the junior locker room. We had both just returned minutes before from a pick-up two-hand touch football game on the junior field. We were sweating and ready for the shower.

Even though I was a half back and did a lot of running during games, I rationalized that I was loosened up enough for a good run.

"Do you want some real competition on a run around St. Joe Lake?" I inquired. Mulkerin was not one to talk excessively. He appeared somewhat receptive to my challenge.

"OK. We can meet outside the house, sometime, and walk over to the lake path. When would you like to do this?"

He seemed way too comfortable with the idea, but seemed tired from the football game..

"How about today, like right now?" I suggested.

"Remember, it's not like the one-mile around St. Mary's Lake, he cautioned. It's at least an extra quarter of a mile." I didn't know that he knew of my running St. Mary's lake.

"Yeah, I know, man. Let's do it," I said.

His long, easy stride on the way to St. Joe's should have raised all the red flags. I was hustling to keep up. We began at a slow, steady jaunt, not trying to get ahead of each other initially. I found little problem keeping up with Mulkerin's pace until we passed the Moreau Seminary pier, about the half-way point I figured. I was winded and hadn't gotten my second breath.

"I think I have something in my tennis shoe. Could you hold on a minute?" I was struggling with my breathing as I slipped off my shoe, shook it, and slipped it back on, tying it quickly and running out ahead of Mulkerin.

As we passed the NROTC pier at the far end of St. Joe's, Mulkerin was several paces ahead, running at what appeared to be a leisurely pace. My shorter legs were churning just to maintain the distance between us. I was desperate for oxygen. I dragged my right foot.

"Whoa! I almost lost my shoe. Hold on a minute," I blurted out hoping he'd heard me and too winded to repeat myself.

Mulkerin stopped once again, returning to where I was hunched down, looking at my shoe. I was too tired and winded to reach down to the shoe. I pushed it along the ground.

"I think I have it," I stammered.

Mulkerin, alert and cool as ever responded, "Are you OK? You know, we don't have to complete this, if you want to stop now." I didn't respond.

I made a desperate attempt to lunge ahead of Mulkerin again. He easily passed me by. I'm sure he knew that my stamina was shot.

We approached the end of the race, with Mulkerin kindly staying a few paces ahead of me. I was thankful, in case there was anyone watching from the junior locker room. As we completed the race--and I use the word "completed" carefully--and were running the final hundred yards or so, Mulkerin broke from the road and took the short-cut across the junior playing field to Holy Cross. I continued on to our starting point, limp and beaten.

Oh! And by the way, Father LeVasseur beat Reyes by half a stride.

PREP SCHOOL DAYS The Seminary at the University of Notre Dame

Courtesy of Jim Glaza-1954

Spud Room, above the Steam House   Andy Roering and Andy Stevans

STEAM MEN

During the bitter cold, windy, and snowy Indiana winters that often began in late September, and continued through May, someone at Holy Cross had to feed the coal furnaces day and night. These hardy souls were designated "Steam Men."

Over a three-year period, Jim Algeo, Andy Roering and I each had steam man responsibilities. The coal furnace, located in a separate building, converted coal heat to steam. The steam was piped underground to Holy Cross house, where it fed radiators, located along walls in every room throughout the immense three story structure.

Algeo, the first steam man I knew, was a senior, originally from Philadelphia. Roering, who assumed my steam man responsibilities the following year, was from Minnesota and knew all about warming fires and cold winters.

The job was interesting and demanding, requiring mandatory watchfulness nine months of the year.

For me steam man responsibilities began when Father Fiedler approached me in the main hallway, accompanied by Algeo. It was during the early fall of my junior year. The weather had turned chilly. Yet the house felt warm and comfortable.

"For your next obedience (house duty) I'd like you to learn to be the Holy Cross steam man. Mr. Algeo, here, will teach you how to maintain the house furnace. Your job will be to heat the house on cold days." Father Fiedler smiled and walked off.

Algeo, a husky, all around athlete, and a tough competitor during the previous month's junior-senior game, smiled and said, "Follow me."

We walked through the large kitchen, circling around a stainless steel dish washing unit that dominated the room, and out to the steam house, a 24 by 24 foot building. The steam house was two stories high with the lower level hidden from the front. The front had two doors, facing the main Holy Cross house across a walking path. From the building's hidden lower level, there was a back exit, facing St. Mary's lake.

I had been through one of the steam house front doors many times. This was where Speltz and I skinned muskrats and dried their pelts, and where three classmates skinned potatoes using an electric rotating machine that resembled a small cement mixer. We called it the "spud machine." The room was nicknamed "the spud room." On the same level, Herman, the caretaker, had a private room accessed from the spud room.

I had not been through the other front door which led down steps to the steam room, below. Algeo opened the door with a key, flipped on a light switch and led me down the steep flight of stairs that ended in a basement.

"This is our steam room, and back here…" he led me toward the back door and pointed to his left into a darkened room; "this is the coal room where you'll shovel coal into the furnace." He reached up and flicked on a small light to show several tons of coal. Our shadows reflected against the far coal room wall.

"Where's the furnace?" I asked.

Algeo smiled through large teeth, and turned back toward the steps. He pointed to the right. Facing the coal room were two, five foot square iron doors. He slipped on leather gloves and threw open the furnace doors. The blast of heat was considerable. Algeo's face lit up, his freckles as bright as the fire in the furnace.

"Do you see this long poker?" With a practiced motion, Algeo grabbed an eight foot iron rod, flattened on the end, and poked it into the fire. The mass of coals suddenly came alive, belching hot flecks of fire that filled the interior of the furnace. Algeo explained that the heat from the burning coal warmed water pipes. The water pipes passed underground and into Holy Cross house.

"That bed of coals has to stay hot. I'll show you how to measure the amount of fresh coal to shovel into the furnace, and how to pack the coal so it gives off a steady heat all night. It has to be repeated again in the morning, early." Algeo pushed the furnace doors shut and latched them.

"The furnace should be checked several times each day. If there's a problem, find Herman, or report it to Father Fiedler." We walked toward the stairs.

"You'd better stay in good physical condition because this monster," he pointed back toward the furnace, "is always hungry. It demands a lot of coal and baby sitting day and night."

The following day, I moved from the junior locker room to a third floor room shared with Algeo. Other rooms were occupied by seniors, many of whom I had forged friendships with during my early summer arrival the previous year.

Several weeks later, I assumed full steam man status and was given the key to the steam house. Algeo remained in the room, but was assigned other house duties.

I visited the steam room as often as possible to check the furnace, but also to pursue the work-out regimen that Klouda and I had begun earlier.

In the morning, following pre-Mass prayers, when many students left the chapel to go to confession, I would leave chapel and go to the steam house. It became a habit that allowed me 15 minutes to stoke, add coal and pack the furnace, and 15 minutes to exercise. I would do the same before sports in the afternoons. Shoveling coal became part of my upper-body routine. Often I would shadow box on the coal shed wall, my shadow enlarged by the dim light bulb.

In my senior year, Father Fiedler introduced me to Andy Roering, from Minnesota. I was to teach Roering what Algeo had taught me: how to be a steam man.

Roering was strong for his size, He possessed a unique, deep, nervous laugh, and had the ruddy, outdoor complexion of a farm hand. His hair always seemed a bit disheveled.

Both Roering and I had a streak of storyteller in us. A favorite subject was farming. A few years before Holy Cross, I had spent a summer and fall working on a small farm south of

Pittsburgh, Pennsylvania, not far from the Holy Cross property at Deep Creek, Maryland.

Farming was a subject close to both of our hearts, particularly the stories about our teen shenanigans that farm life provided. I promised myself then and there I would record some of my farm stories in a book, a promise that took many years to accomplish.

It was late in my senior year when I learned that Father O'Donnell and Father Van Wolvlear performed daily exercises in their rooms. They were big on pushups, squats, side-straddle hops and running in place, each exercise a part of my own regimen.

**The first snow, front lawn of Holy Cross, Notre Dame, 1953
Looking toward the Holy Cross entrance, the Grotto & Dome**

ICEMAN, FUNNYMAN

Eddie Donovan, dressed in black suit, black tie and white shirt, walked with a short powerful stride, his body lurching forward like a professional weight lifter preparing to reach for the weights. He moved up the aisle quickly and climbed the steps to the stage.

It was the monthly movie evening at Holy Cross and everyone was anxiously awaiting Mr. Donovan's often hilarious reading of the "Minutes of the Mission Society."

He would begin something like, "Father LeVasseur almost fell down when I expressed my interest in the Mission Society. Let me explain his surprise. Father and I are from the deep south, New Orleans, and down there we have a tradition of moving slow so we don't suffer heat stroke. This assignment offered me a New Orleans "slow," so I immediately jumped at the opportunity. I must admit it has allowed me to avoid study halls several times each month."

Donovan was as much admired for his sense of humor as for his strength. He respected anyone who attempted to stay in good condition. Much of his own conditioning was earned the hard way, carrying ice.

In order to help support his family, Donovan spent his days delivering ice used to cool the old fashioned "ice boxes," found in neighborhoods throughout New Orleans. Today, we think of ice as a bag of pre-formed ice cubes weighing no more than 10 pounds. Donovan carried blocks of ice a full cubic foot in size. He'd throw a soft leather pad across his shoulders and, with leather gloves and ice hooks, mount a block of ice on his shoulder, walking to each customer's home on a busy ice delivery route. I'm pretty sure that most of Donovan's days were not a New Orleans "slow".

Because of his strength he toned down his sports play at Holy Cross, yet he could maneuver surprisingly fast in football, and was a wiry and agile competitor.

Donovan was two years ahead of me, in my brother, Norm's class. Norm commented on Donovan's humility and kindness, and his difficulty with studies. Norm described him as a warm and decent guy who loved Holy Cross.

Bernie Manale, one year behind my Holy Cross class of 1955, also grew up in New Orleans. In fact he lived around the corner from Donovan and, like Donovan, attended Sts. Peter and Paul Grammar School, run by the Marionite Sisters of Holy Cross—"a tough bunch," according to Manale.

"I discovered Holy Cross because Donovan went there," Manale said.

PARENTS: VISITING SUNDAYS

Every student anticipated Visiting Sundays in the fall and spring. Some seminarians had no visitors at all. I presumed that, like Sowala, some returned home to their local families. I recall Jim Glaza, and Tom Hayes and his older brother, John, had visitors from Michigan, probably as often as I did. But, there were always many family visitors to Holy Cross. The parents tried to include some of the students who had no visitors. I was fortunate that, dad, after years of working on the railroad, was presented with a Golden Pass, free passage for him and the family on the Pittsburgh and Lake Erie (New York Central) Railroad. The pass was honored by the Penn Central and other railroads as well.

The Golden Pass almost guaranteed fall and spring visits from family and younger siblings. I could also count on gifts of candy bars and other treats, and for my April birthday, a homemade pineapple-upside-down cake, a lifelong favorite.

To classmates it appeared I could produce sweets at any time throughout the year. I explained simply that my folks were very giving people.

PREP SCHOOL DAYS The Seminary at the University of Notre Dame

Never-the-less, on this late date I can finally admit to my strategy. Instead of sending dirty laundry to the Notre Dame laundromat, I mailed mine home every 10 days. Inside the returned laundry container I received clean, folded clothes, candy bars and other edibles. The word did get out. I blame my generous nature. My nickname changed from "Pierre" (the lumberjack) to "Stash."

Dad was attracted to the lake and the surrounding woods. Much like Father Fiedler, dad had farming and the outdoors in his blood. He demonstrated how mushrooms growing on a fallen tree were edible. At Holy Cross, I never had the opportunity to build a camp fire and cook eggs, bacon, and mushrooms over a fire. That exercise was reserved for summer hikes and camping back home.

On Visiting Sundays mom would always ask to visit with Sister Zacharia--"Sister Zack" as we students had nick named her--and Sister Mary Amata. Sister Zacharia was a heavy-set, solid woman. Both Sisters were cooks for Holy Cross House. Their ability to deliver daily satisfying meals to a few hundred people, a majority comprised of growing, hungry young men, was awe inspiring. Sister St. Rita, another pleasant, no nonsense nun, was the house nurse. She was infirmarian, dispensarian, and the final word on any illness. I benefited more than once from her medical remedies.

On one visit I remember Mom and Sister Zacharia entertaining each other for some time with stories of growing up, mom in a small college town in Pennsylvania and Sister Zacharia in a small town in Austria. They spoke at length about the war years. Mom had lost her only brother, a marine aviator, in the Pacific. I recall one dark story that Sister Zacharia related of her and Sister Mary Amata's families' plights in Germany during the World Wars, the forced labor, fighting, and family deaths and suffering. Both women, mom and Sister, were strong individuals, able to handle the pain of relating these sad memories without breaking down

On the lighter side, mom always inquired about Sister's parakeet. They would fawn over "Budgie bird" each visit. I experienced a relaxed, happier side to Sister Zacharia, a side she seldom displayed toward us students; those of us working the dishwasher or having obedience assignments in other parts of the kitchen. We were expected to do exactly as Sister Zacharia requested. If you demonstrated cooperation and were hard working, Sister referred to you as Hans ("Hanz"), an almost sacred title with Sister Zacharia. Before being assigned to kitchen duty, I heard the rumor that, if you landed on Sister's bad side, you suffered the terrible penance of being labeled "Fritz," almost forever. In fairness to Sister Zacharia, I should mention that I probably transferred the stern natures of the Sisters of Charity, back home, onto Sister Zacharia.

But, thinking back, maybe I did make a few points with Sister Zacharia. During the parent's final visit before my graduation, I related a kitchen incident to them. As a new obedience, I had been placed in charge of the dishwasher operation. At that time, I was probably in my best physical condition while at Holy Cross.

One of my kitchen duties was to load two five-gallon milk containers into the milk dispensers that stood several feet off the floor. As I reached down and began to lift one of the five gallon containers, Sister Zacharia appeared out of nowhere.

"Here, Hanz, let me do that. You'll hurt your self." Sister lifted the first five- gallon milk container easily with one hand, and shifted it into place in the dispenser. She quickly lifted the second five gallon milk container, and juggled it into position next to the first, then disappeared back into the pantry. I stood quietly for a moment, admiring what I'd just seen and trying not to laugh over the whole thing.

I can safely say that without the positive influence of the Sisters of Notre Dame at Holy Cross, all of us boys would have been a lot poorer and most likely a lot thinner for the experience.

THE SOIREE

Save for the chapel and the refectory, I hadn't seen as large a gathering of house priests in my two years at Holy Cross. It was late in my junior year. A large hole had been dug by Herman, the groundskeeper, with the help of several seniors. The hole was located behind the Butler building, a new classroom and gym facility, and next to the short gravel road leading to the priest cemetery.

I soon discovered it was a fire pit. It measured at least 8 feet across and a yard deep. Frs. Riley, Fiedler, Brinker, Simmons and several others were supervising the effort. A crew comprised of a few priests with rolled-up sleeves and several seniors, scrambled to build a layer of corn leaves and silk stripped from fresh ears of corn. On top of that layer, they placed ears of corn. This process continued until there were several layers approximately four-foot square in the center of the pit.

After finishing with the corn, the crew wrapped unskinned potatoes in tin foil to make the top and final layer. I didn't observe what other food they had deposited in the fire pit, but soon a wood stack was carefully built over the layered food and a fire ignited. Everyone stepped back to view the spectacle. The group dispersed for a planned rendezvous later that afternoon.

I accompanied some of my junior classmates walking toward the priest's cemetery entrance. Several yards short of the entrance and to the left of the foot path stood a deserted, wooden, two-story barn. The doors were padlocked. Glancing inside we noticed an old cider press set up near the door. We wondered if Sister Zacharia knew of the cider press and the possibility of fresh apple juice for the entire house. Jerry Wood mentioned that the cider press probably belonged to Herman, the grounds keeper—his secret.

We imagined Herman stashing apples from the trees nearby, and making hard cider by aging the unfiltered, unpasteurized pressed apples. Dave Gibson or Tom Norris may have brought up the fact that you could age corn in similar fashion to make corn liquor. We were getting into forbidden territory with these comments, and so continued walking.

We stopped at the cemetery fence. Jon Lullo commented that ground squirrels (Chipmunks) made nests under the grave stones, causing the stones to fall over. He showed us a hose hooked up to a water supply, inside the cemetery. Apparently, several of the juniors, Jon Lullo, Norm Lakatos, and a few others made it their mission to drown the chipmunks out of the cemetery, permanently. I heard that the effort paid off, at least during our tenure at Holy Cross.

After the short walk, the group broke up. I returned to the seminary building. Once inside I walked down the main corridor. I heard quick footsteps approaching from behind. Father Banas, my spiritual advisor at the time, appeared to be on a mission as he bolted up the slate steps toward the second floor, only to lose his footing halfway up.

"Dammit," he mumbled, getting back to his feet.

I had cursed many times in the distant past, but this was an opportunity that couldn't be ignored. Besides, Father Banas was caught cursing in front of an impressionable, young seminarian.

"Father, what are you damning?" I asked.

Father turned toward me, almost losing his balance again.

"It's all right to damn an inanimate object," he managed to say, as he turned and continued his hectic pace up the stairs. It seemed like a perfectly logical and acceptable answer. Priests seem particularly adept at providing well grounded answers to profound philosophical inquiry.

After a short time at study, I grew hungry. Others had left the study hall. I joined some of them, and returned to the fire-pit to collect the hot corn-on-the-cob then join classmates at the picnic tables, set up earlier near the St. Mary's Lake pier. The outdoor luncheon or "soirée" as we called it had its own form of excitement, as I would soon find out.

It hadn't taken but a short few hours for the fire to die down. The remaining smoking embers were removed and the food exposed. We lined up with plates to sample the freshly baked corn and potatoes. I talked Father Fiedler out of two large cobs and one Idaho potato and hurried down to the lake front where beans and hamburgers were being served from one of the picnic tables. I selected two large prepared hamburgers, added a few dippers of beans, and drowned the cobs of sweet corn and the potato in liquefied butter.

With the food dish in one hand and a large orange drink in the other, I walked several paces toward the lake to join a classmate, Bob Kuker, and several others sitting in the grass. Kuker matched me bite for bite as we talked about the superb flavor of the corn-on-the-cob. I told Kuker about a corn-on-the-cob eating contest (back then we called it a "corntest") I had won when I was 14, mentioning that this was the first corn-on-the-cob I'd been able to stomach since.

A half hour later, following some discussion and a lot more eating, Kuker and I had that bug-eyed look that all over-eaters suffer. We decided to walk around the lake to ease our discomfort, making it as far as Norm and my Weeping Willow tree—our earlier melon-eating spot. Kuker and I managed to climb out on a limb. We hoped for a belch-- something, anything--to relieve the agony of our gluttony.

After what seemed like several excruciating hours, I walked back to Holy Cross House, short cutting through the kitchen next to the barber shop. Sowala was waiting to give me a haircut. It was the day he'd discover my first grey hair, not as memorable an event as I put on, since pre-mature grey hair existed in my family.

Yet, overall, the day of the soiree turned out to be an exceptional learning experience. I learned how to set up an outdoor fire pit and bake corn-on-the-cob and potatoes. I learned there was an apple press on the property. I learned that priests curse at inanimate objects. And I learned the serious consequences of practicing the cardinal sin of gluttony.

Andrew Stevans

...JUNIOR YEAR...

(Courtesy of Jerry Wood, Photo by Jim Keating)
Tom Hayes, Jerry Wood, Bob Kuker, 1954

CSMC

In late August at the beginning of our junior year at Holy Cross, there was an invasion of sorts. From across the country a group of high school students, mostly young women, descended onto the campus of Notre Dame, each representing their parish at the Catholic Student Mission Crusade (CSMC), a youth mission support effort created many years before by a group of missionary nuns.

A number of CSMC girls appeared one evening near the St. Mary's lake pier, and thus near the locker rooms of Holy Cross. We seminarians soon discovered the girls were everywhere, infesting (in the nicest way possible) the entire Notre Dame campus. Holy Cross was not overlooked.

We took the matter in stride. Jon Lullo, who may have known one of the CSMC ladies, along with several other juniors and seniors explained that Holy Cross was a men's seminary and there was a protocol for visitors—or lack of it, I was never sure.

Unfortunately, the guys at Holy Cross and the girls from CSMC were about the same age, and our kind efforts extended to escorting them to the seminary grounds entrance, then over to the grotto, then onto main campus, and then… There were no casualties. All of our juniors and seniors were accounted for at evening chapel.

Andrew Stevans

WALKING WOUNDED
JUNIOR-SENIOR FOOTBALL GAME

The Holy Cross Junior-Senior football game was an annual tradition, held each August before the arrival of freshmen and sophomores. We juniors were skilled athlete's and confident in our knowledge of the game and our ability to win. The summer vacation had produced some big seniors. To me, the line looked like Notre Dame's first string.

Our junior team had a few husky lads, but, in general, we were a lighter, faster, stronger group of competitors, and decided to rely on our maneuverability to win the game. Sowala, our quarterback, asked me to play end, facing John Massart, from Chicago. Massert had me by at least 20 pounds. He was a strong competitor and fast on his feet.

Our team was soon ahead by one touchdown, and we had possession of the ball. Sowala fell back looking to throw a long pass. I advanced quickly, attempting to get around Massart and go long for the pass. My tibia and knee collided with Massart's on his forward drive. I dropped to the ground in pain, and, after some help, managed to limp to the sidelines. For a short while, I was unaware of the game. The pain was intense. Frs. Fiedler and Brinker came over to look at the injured knee. I was urged to sit out the rest of the game. Our junior team won easily.

A group of us had planned to take a swim in St. Joe Lake following the game. The knee felt somewhat better, so I joined the group, and limped around the western end of St. Joe Lake to the Moreau Seminary pier. I dove into the waters hoping to cool the hot and swollen knee. After 15 minutes the knee became stiff. I barely made it back to Holy Cross in time to dress for chapel and dinner. I should have reported to the dispensary and let Sister St. Rita work her magic, but an unnecessary bravado drove me on.

For most of that night, I remained awake with knee pain. By morning I couldn't put weight on the leg and remained in bed. Following an agonizing few hours, I managed to limp to Father Langendorfer's door to ask for help. Father Fiedler arrived in minutes and, after consultation with Sister St. Rita, recommended transfer to the Notre Dame Infirmary. I remember the short ride to the infirmary primarily because of the difficulty getting in and out of the car. I can't remember how I got into the infirmary or into bed.

The infirmary doctor ordered hot compresses applied to the knee day and night. He described the injury as "a direct trauma to the medial aspect of the tibia." I would find out several days later that the doctor's orders for hot compresses should have been cold compresses.

During the several days spent at the Notre Dame infirmary, I met an elderly priest, Father Owens, who visited each day. The second day of my stay, he brought by a book he had read, "The Dead Sea Scrolls." I had always enjoyed reading, and the subject of the book kept my mind off the painful knee. Each day that Father visited, we had interesting conversations about the mystery of the scrolls and what I had read.

In the early morning of my fifth day at the infirmary, a different doctor came into the room, took a look at the knee, and ordered my immediate transport to St. Joe Hospital. At St. Joe, the knee was drained and I was given instruction on the use of crutches.

Later that afternoon, I was allowed to return to Holy Cross. I soon became adept at hopping around using only one crutch, and going up and down stairs with ease. This ability would serve me well in later years following leg injuries suffered on the playing field, and while serving aboard ship in the Atlantic Fleet.

SISTER ST. RITA'S DISPENSARY

The Holy Cross dispensary fell under the jurisdiction of Sister St. Rita. Sister was a scant five-feet tall, tiny to us growing young men. She maintained a pleasant but firm disposition. Sister could display a strict demeanor that reminded me of the fearsome elementary and high school Sisters of Charity, back home.

Never-the-less, what Sister St. Rita managed to do so well, possibly without being aware of it, was to provide us a place of refuge, away from the playing field, away from the discipline and obediences, and away from the study regimen at Holy Cross.

If we had a sore throat, a cut or abrasion, or suffered any ache or pain, then, following final chapel in the evening, we were expected to go to the dispensary. Sister St. Rita addressed a long line of complainants each evening. I was one of them.

"Next in line, please." At least several dozen times during my three years at Holy Cross, Sister swabbed a sore throat with Sweet Methiolate, or disinfected a cut or abrasion with Mercurochrome or a dab of anti-biotic cream and a patch.

The dispensary, a twelve by six foot room, was meticulous. The painted floor always looked freshly cleaned. Sister's medicines and supplies were stored in a white cabinet with a glass front. In addition, a small table held an open bottle of sweet methiolate, and a clear glass bottle filled with cotton balls. Next to the glass bottle stood a stainless steel container holding a large supply of swabs. The room also contained a study hall chair where you sat if Sister decided to bandage a larger wound or to give an injection.

It seemed that most of us were there with sore throats, so received the throat swab remedy. Often, one of us would require a band aid or larger gauze pad for a scratch or cut. These simple first aid solutions were administered as we stood just outside the dispensary door.

"Next in line, please," became Sister St. Rita's rallying cry to the student body.

I remember Ed LeMasse, a senior from Chicago, holding up the line for at least 20 minutes. Sister wanted to administer a needle into his lower right arm. LeMasse, a tough, wiry competitor on the playing field, was sitting down, resting his elbow on the study hall chair, his arm bent. Every time Sister attempted to push in the needle, it broke. Sister smiled, determined, and produced a larger needle. After several tries Sister had success. LeMasse left the dispensary red faced and shaken.

Early in my junior year, I was sitting in study hall after a particularly competitive football game. During the game, I had caught several long passes and performed kick-offs. Following the game I felt beat but pushed myself to do a lap around St. Mary's Lake.

It came on fast, the old rheumatic pains in my knees that I had experienced during the lost summer with rheumatic fever, following my fifth grade. Shortly, I was unable to tolerate the aching and went to the Sisters' quarters asking for Sister St. Rita. Sister listened quietly, and asked me to wait in the nuns' guest room. Upon her return she had a large glass of cold water and a small paper envelope containing a dozen or so pills. Sister called them APCs.

"Take three now, and two with a full glass of water every four hours—and no football or excessive running tomorrow. I'll see you at the dispensary this evening and tomorrow evening." I was ushered out of the Sisters' quarters.

In my estimation, the APCs were a miracle drug. Shortly after taking the pills, there was absolutely no knee pain. It would be a few years later that I rediscovered APCs in the Navy. I discovered they were a combination of Aspirin, Phenacetin, and Caffeine, a reliable pain killer similar to, but in my experience more effective and quicker acting, than Excedrin.

During the early 1980's, my daughter attended Notre Dame Academy in Middleburg, VA. On her first day at the academy, who came to greet my wife and family but Sister St. Rita. One of the first remarks Sister made was that I visited the dispensary too much at Holy Cross.

"I think that was my brother, Jack, Sister. We look alike," I blurted out, surprised at Sister's recall.

"No, it was you Andrew. Your brother Norman introduced you to me." How do you fight a statement like that? I didn't remember being introduced by Norm, but I decided this was one of those lose-lose situations. I shut up, and Sister continued on,

"You and Mr. Zahradnik were my noisiest patients when you both were sick in the infirmary." I smiled, realizing that I would have to tell someone that story some day.

Anyone who met Sister St. Rita would not easily forget her kind and giving nature. Tom Hayes had an expression for stellar humans. He referred to them as "Archangels." That perfectly describes Sister St. Rita.

QUARANTINED

During the spring of my junior year, I caught a flu-like bug. Up to Sister St. Rita's dispensary I went, weak and fevered.

"You'll have to move to the infirmary for a few days." Sister said.

I retrieved my bathrobe and slippers and shaving kit, and then reported to the dispensary. Sister led me to the infirmary. She opened the door and allowed me to enter, pointing me toward a bed. I discovered that a senior, Ray Zahradnik, had also been admitted to the infirmary.

Zahradnik was also from Pennsylvania. A year earlier, he was a sophomore monitor. Many times he had helped me solve geometry problems in the hall mop closet outside the study hall.

Apparently we both suffered from the same symptoms.

"You look pretty sick," he managed to say, smiling, tucked in under several layers of sheets and blankets. I was shivering and unable to do other than greet Zahradnik with a mumble. I remember nothing more until the following morning. Zahradnik was sitting on the side of his bed, holding his head.

"Don't worry about the fever and shakes, that's short-lived. The headache and coughing are the killers." He attempted a laugh, ending up with a hacking cough.

"Sister St. Rita will heal us with one of her miracle cures," I managed to respond, lost in my own pain and misery. Later in the day, we both felt somewhat better, but concluded that we'd been placed in quarantine. At that point, we decided to make the best of it.

Like me, Zahradnik loved the sports at Holy Cross. He was a strong football and basketball player, probably a natural athlete. Some of his teammates viewed him as a one-man team on the basketball court, not necessarily a good thing for his team. He was an exceptional receiver and lineman on the football field.

For the next few days, we talked not only sports, Holy Cross and attending the at-home Notre Dame football games, but branched out into philosophical discussions of living the spiritual life among the priests and seminarians.

I remember bringing up the subject of the parochial school system in Pittsburgh and the tough, no nonsense Sisters of Charity. I included a few negative incidents that happened, nuns versus students, in elementary school. Zahradnik matched me with a few elementary school stories if his own. We both had good laughs over the incidents.

Sister St. Rita monitored our meals and, at least once, commented on our behavior—laughing and talking too loud. We apologized with promises to "keep it down." Sister smiled and disappeared back into the hallway.

Zahradnik mentioned his home town of Ford City, Pennsylvania, and the Ford City High School college scholarships available to graduating seniors. I recall he was genuinely interested in what Ford City High School had to offer its seniors.

Considering all the silence periods we as seminarians followed in day-to-day life at Holy Cross, Zahradnik and I had much chatter to make up for. And over those few days in Sister St. Rita's infirmary, we easily made up for a year's worth of silences.

Each day we had meals delivered from the kitchen with Sister overseeing the food served. We suffered hacking coughs and minor breathing problems. Sister checked up on us several times each day, taking vital signs.

Zahradnik left the dispensary a day before I did.

"How do you plan to catch up on studies?" I asked, always concerned about what I had missed in classes. Zahradnik laughed, and after a short fit of coughing and clearing his throat responded.

"I plan to go to the rec room during the afternoon break and read physics. That's the only one I'll have to catch up on. The rest are easy." He then entertained me with stories about putting teachers on guard with debate-type questions and simple logic. I began to realize why he was able to solve my geometry problems so easily.

Sister discharged me the following day, in time for lunch. Following lunch, I short cut through the senior rec room to attend a class at the new Butler building, next door. Sure enough, there was Zahradnik, lounging in an easy chair, reading through his physics book and carrying on a conversation with a classmate. Later, I asked how difficult subjects came to him so easily. He smiled,

"I think it's my IQ. I'm told it's 180."

Years later I discovered that Zahradnik had obtained a full scholarship undergraduate degree, and a masters and doctorate in Chemical Engineering from Carnegie Tech (now, Carnegie Mellon), then went on to head the chemical division of a large petroleum company.

I think Sister St. Rita's medicine saved the life of a natural athlete and brilliant scholar. She also saved mine.

Andrew Stevans

KITCHEN SUPPORT
THE GREASE TRAP

It was late one afternoon on a weekend. Several of my classmates and I had returned from Washington Hall, after attending Notre Dame's student stage play "Serendipity." We hummed show tunes, laughed about some of the scenes and discussed the professionalism of the actors. It was an enjoyable play and a welcome break from the strict regimen of life at Holy Cross. We decided to walk through the dishwasher room, and down a side hall to see what was going on in the senior rec room.

I had recently been assigned a new obedience in the kitchen, a daily task after each meal, monitoring the soap levels and water heat levels as three classmates and I fed several hundred dishes, bowls, cups and silverware into the 30 foot long, stainless steel behemoth.

Sister Zacharia appeared from the kitchen cooking area, smiling, beckoning to me. I should have sensed trouble and been on guard.

"How queasy is your stomach, Hanz?" Sister Zacharia smiled again. She carried a long spoon-like metal rod and a small shovel. Her large frame blocked the sun reflecting off the stainless steel dishwasher, the rays absorbed into Sister's white robes.

"Sister, I don't think I have a queasy stomach."

"Good, follow me." It was a direct order. I obediently followed Sister. She walked around the perimeter of the dishwasher, and out the side door into the cool spring evening. Sister pointed to a door and a short set of stairs, located near the entrance to the Sister's quarters. I followed her into a small cellar that ended at a wall directly beneath the dish washing room, above.

"See the plate in the floor? Here, I show you how to do this. Watch how I open the grease-trap." Sister was huffing and puffing as she leaned over with the long metal rod, and inserted it into an 18 inch metal plate built into the basement floor. With a single twist of her wrist, the plate came loose. The smell from old grease and other putrification that arose from the hole made me catch my breath.

"I'll let you clean it out, Hanz. Bring over an empty coffee can."

Sister pointed toward some empty, several gallon coffee cans stacked against the basement wall.

"You clean by pulling up the trap, slowly, and emptying the old grease into a coffee can. Also, use this small shovel to clean anything remaining from the bottom or the sludge will back up into the kitchen dishwasher. It must be done every Saturday."

"I understand Sister." I cleaned the grease trap quickly, and picked up the half full coffee can.

"You put the collected grease next to the dumpster on the side of the steam house. It is picked up each week."

"Yes Sister, OK." I was anxious to get rid of the can as quickly as possible.

Upon returning from the dumpster, Sister Zack was standing outside the kitchen door.

"Very good, Hanzie; come, I show you where to put the tools." I followed Sister back into the kitchen.

"Every Saturday morning, Hanz; and tomorrow, I show you how to clean the cook stove with a brush." Sister disappeared through the kitchen, into the Sister's quarters.

I continued on my way to the senior rec room. I wondered what I would tell my classmates to explain the smell on my clothes, and the meeting with Sister Zack. I tried to get my mind off the grease-trap's sludge smell by humming one of the show tunes from "Serendipity."

"It was just another day; started out the same old way..." I felt queasy in the stomach and realized it wasn't just another day.

SPUD KINGS

For some reason that is lost to memory, three classmates, Norris, Lullo and Vogel, all from Chicago, were nicknamed "The Piggies clique." They sometimes met in the spud house to discuss home town sports events and other Chicago trivia. Two of the three were the spud kings of Holy Cross, so meeting in the spud house was a natural. Vogel's and Lullo's daily obedience was to provide Sister Zacharia with clean, peeled potatoes. Their method was to load a spud machine with potatoes in a rinse of water. The final result was dozens of cleanly peeled potatoes ready for cooking, or baking. Norris, a true man of action, probably helped build the spud kings' reputations during these talk sessions.

The spud operation was located on the upper level of the steam house and directly across a dirt and gravel road from the entrance door to the kitchen. The machine that did 90% of the work, built similar to a small cement mixer, contained a rotating, abrasive metal tub. When rotated with a few dozen potatoes inside the spud machine would quickly scrape each potato clean of peels to emerge ready for re-washing—and the spud kings' careful inspection. Another batch of a few dozen would be washed, dumped into the machine, and the operation would begin again, until several tall stainless pots were filled with perfectly cleaned, peeled potatoes.

Sister Zach was intolerant when it came to laziness, and wouldn't accept dirty or partially peeled spuds. Since Norris, Lullo and Vogel were fastidious in their potato peeling duties, they were guaranteed a good association with Sister—and probably endless spud room chat sessions about their home town.

I think the spud operation could have been theirs indefinitely, if it weren't for Father Fiedler's and Father LeVasseur's occasional assignment of new obediences. Soon they were off doing daily refectory table waiting, or barbering, or cleaning locker rooms. The home town sports discussions were then confined to the playing field, to meals, or to the recreation room. The Chicago "Piggies clique" remained close friends well beyond Holy Cross.

EATING WILD VENISON

I don't know who shot the deer. It was a big one, at least 150 pounds, certainly enough to feed everyone at Holy Cross. No one noticed the dead deer until after breakfast. It hung from a rope near the spud room door.

Sometime during the day, the dead deer disappeared, and we anticipated eating venison (deer meat) for dinner soon. Someone commented on the wild taste of venison if it wasn't marinated properly.

My Uncle John owned a farm, north of Pittsburgh, in the Cook Forest area in Pennsylvania. During the fall, he'd marinate, braise, cook in gravy then bottle in Ball jars many quarts of venison that he and Aunt Mary would consume throughout the winter months. He called it simply "Bottled Bucks Meat." We called it "Uncle John's deer stew." The stew contained absolutely no taste of the wild. It was flavorful and delicious, the best meat stew I've tasted.

On one of our summer breaks from Holy Cross, my brother Norm and I bicycled the hundred miles to the farm to help Uncle John mow his wheat and oat fields. In all truthfulness, it was a journey to taste his deer stew, and to bring a jar or two home with us.

Uncle John hung on to most of his Bottled Bucks Meat, so it was considered a rarity to see a few jars of the famous stew at the local county fair. We heard that a bottle sold for $3.00. Uncle John would match his price to the price of a pint of home made piccalilli, another popular item at the annual county fair.

At Holy Cross, one afternoon, the venison was served hot and tender, thanks to Sister Zacharia's cooking skills. But the meat had an acidic taste, as though it had been prepared in apple vinegar. I ate some of it, just to say I'd tried it. Most of my table mates ate little or none at all. I thought of Uncle John preparing his bottled buck's meat with a wild taste still evident in the venison. He would not be proud.

(Courtesy of Jerry Wood; Photo by Jim Keating)
Aunt Eller (Tom Norris), Jud (Gerry Matheny) and Curly (Tom Hayes)

MUSICALS, HOLY CROSS STYLE

"*G*eese and Ducks and Chicks Better Scurry..."

"Oklahoma" was my second stage play. The first, at St. James High, back home in Pittsburgh, was a rendition of "When in Ireland, Do as the Irish Do."

At Holy Cross, we were lucky to have Father Simmons from the Notre Dame Department of Classics to supervise and support the staging of "Oklahoma."

"Oh, what a beautiful mornin',
Oh what a beautiful day..."

Hayes played Curly, probably the first bass to play the part. His strong rendition of "Surry with the fringe on top" and his strutting around the stage brought down the house.

Glaza played Will,

"Ev'rythin's up to date in Kansas City;
They've gone about as fur as they c'n go!"

It was obvious from Glaza's Two-Step that he was the perfect pick for the part.

I was Sheriff Andrew Carnes, attempting to be the voice of reason between farmers and cowmen,

"One man likes to push a plough,
The other likes to chase a cow,
But that's no reason why they cain't be friends."

Our group spent many days learning to square dance. Of course in a seminary, men had to dress as women. Aunt Eller was played by Norris, who was well over six feet tall, probably the tallest Aunt Eller to ever grace the stage.

Callahan had acting in his blood. Not only was he Ado Annie in Oklahoma, he also played Buttercup in Gilbert & Sullivan's "H.M.S. Pinafore." In that Savoy operetta, Speltz played the love sick sailor, Ralph.

"She laughs my love to scorn,
yet I adore her."

Ralph was hopelessly in love with the captain's daughter, Josephine.

"Refrain audacious tar, your suite from pressing.
Remember who you are and whom addressing."

Unfortunately, I don't recall who played the part of Josephine.

"*I am the Captain of the Pinafore,
and a right good Captain too,*"

Hayes, with his bass tones, gave a powerful rendition of Captain Corcoran's song. In fact, if the two musicals were rated on gusto alone, Hayes would have won hands down..

Because of the dual roles of men playing men and men playing women, Holy Cross's renditions of the light operas "Oklahoma" and "H.M.S. Pinafore" were comedies within comedies. Yet, both musicals had exceptional period costumes, a professional quality to the acting, and outstanding stage scenes. Gelven, Speltz and I, the scenery painters, will attest to the later.

The effort to produce the two light operas often became intense since, in addition to our class study demands, we had line memorization that required 100% mental application. Then, there were dancing classes in the movie hall, also known as "the Cave," located under the refectory, upstairs, where we ate our meals.

The effort expended on the dance routines and the fact that Father Simmons, a priest, acted as one square dance director often became hilarious. Once the routines were mastered, some of us continued to practice—the Promenade, the Allemande Right and Allemande Left, the Do-Si-Do--in the recreation room, in the classrooms before classes, and on the basketball court before—and sometimes during--games.

Both musicals were staged to entertain our parents, the house priests, and a few others from Notre Dame. But I'm sure that, during the preparation, we entertained ourselves far more than we ever entertained our guests.

Andrew Stevans

It brings a smile of satisfaction just thinking of those two light operas, done up Holy Cross style. To many of us, the memories are right up there in importance with our four-part a capella choir, our team sports and anything else we accomplished during our years at Holy Cross.

(Oklahoma)
Sheriff Andrew Carnes (Andy Stevans)

FATHER ED SHEA, MR. CODY
and French Leçons

"VOgel, what did I just say?" There was a hard sound to the first syllable and an upswing on the final syllable. Ron Vogel's name was delivered with a cynical, slightly nasal quality in Father Shea's baritone. It was our junior year, and first year French. Ron Vogel, from Chicago, was caught asleep at his desk.

Father Shea had a matter-of-fact delivery in class. There was no levity, no joke telling that I remember, just the facts, and only the facts. Still, Father was a gifted and experienced teacher.

Father Shea was probably a typical Holy Cross priest athlete, found not only at Notre Dame, but throughout the congregation of Holy Cross. We had heard that he played a formidable game of tennis. Like most stories about Holy Cross's teaching priests, the story vs. the actual skill had to be tested. One example was Henry Reyes dare and the resulting foot race between Reyes and Father Larry LeVasseur. But it was a rare experience to see Father Shea on the playing fields or out of the classroom. I imagined his university teaching schedule was demanding.

In the fall of the following year, two teams of us seniors had a pick-up basketball game on the outdoor half-courts, near St. Mary's lake. Father Shea walked by. He was most likely walking around the lake saying his Office prayers. Father offered to play for a few minutes. He was shorter than most of us. I thought he would be easy to guard. We seniors had played as a team many times before. Yet, it seemed impossible to guard or contain Father Shea. He made basket after basket—and he was wearing a cassock. We gained a new respect for Father Shea, and he tolerated us.

"VOgel, give me the English translation of my sentence, and repeat it in French, please." Father Shea expected nothing from Vogel. He put his hands in his cassock pockets and began pacing in front of the class.

Vogel, red-faced from his sleep, appeared disoriented.

"Forgive me, Father, for I have sinned. Pardonnez-moi, mon pere, car j'ai peche."

The class burst into laughter. Vogel's response was perfectly correct.

"Father, I apologize for falling asleep, again." More laughter.

That was pure Vogel.

"Is that all you have to say? Vogel, you're useless. Go back to sleep. You seem to learn better that way." Father Shea tried valiantly to hide a smile.

Vogel was caught sleeping a few other times in Fr, Shea's French class, but the amazing subconscious mind of the man always had the translation. Vogel was surely meant for great things.

We had Mr. Cody for our second year of French. He was in his 40's, tall and long legged. In three seconds flat, he would travel the several yards from classroom door to desk and set his books down. He walked quickly and spoke quickly.

From door to desk he blurted out the "Hail Mary," in French. Not the words: "Je vous salue Marie," but the entire first half of the prayer:

PREP SCHOOL DAYS The Seminary at the University of Notre Dame

"Je vous salue Marie, pleine de grâce, le Seigneur est avec toi, tu es bénie entre les femmes et béni est le fruit de tes entrailles, Jésus."

We were to respond with the final half of the prayer:

"St.e Marie, Mère de Dieu, priez pour nous pauvres pécheurs, maintenant et à l'heure de notre mort, ainsi soit-il."

Of course on the first day, we didn't know what he was talking about. Even the savvy French speakers in the class, scholars Tom Norris and Jerry Wood were taken off guard.

Mr. Cody patiently explained our response:

"When I enter the room, I would like you to respond:

'St.e Marie,... Mère de Dieu,.. Priez pour nous pauvres pécheurs,... maintenant et à l'heure... de notre mort... ainsi soit-il."

I heard the scholars scratching mightily on their note pads. I followed their lead. In later classes I chose a chair in the front row near the door hoping, at his height, Mr. Cody would overlook me and my pronunciation of French. It was my only defense.

In all truthfulness I did learn some French that year, as well as the chain of sounds that made up the response to Mr. Cody's "Je vous salue Marie."

Following my years at Holy Cross, I visited Cannes France, Gulfe Juan France, and Monaco, all at the expense of the U.S. Navy. I spoke my best high school French. No one understood, not even the French orphans at the Bishop's on-board orphan's party when I asked them in French to sit down, "assisez vous ici," as I recall. And I still couldn't pray the Hail Mary in real French.

Mr. Cody, like Father Shea was a good teacher. But it would be many years later that my brother, Norm, who had taken advanced French at Duquesne University, replaced my gibberish of French sounds with the actual French words to the Hail Mary. Please don't ask me to repeat them.

Teaching Latin... Father Fiedler approached me late in my junior year.

"Mr. Counihan is struggling with his Latin. Can you take some time and review what he knows and what he doesn't know." Father didn't order me, but simply asked if I could help a fellow student.

"Father, I'll try."

I also had trouble with first year Latin, but later, when advanced Latin class was combined with first-year French--a language related to Latin—things seemed to fall into place.

For an hour after dinner each evening, Bob Counihan and I met in one of the classrooms at the Butler Building. Initially we talked about parts of speech in English. Then, using his Latin book we reviewed declensions and conjugations, cum clauses, and so forth. On the board I demonstrated how various parts of speech fit together and relied on one another in Latin sentences.

In addition to reviewing English to Latin translations in Counihan's Latin book, occasionally, we studied sentence structure and endings in the Daily Missal, in preparation for the following day's Latin Mass. Counihan showed a genuine interest in this approach and his understanding grew rapidly.

I'm sure that my satisfaction—and fascination--from seeing a student learn a subject following my directions, far outweighed Counihan's satisfaction with learning.

Father Fiedler had launched me on a teaching quest I would follow for most of my adult life.

FATHER WILLIAM LYONS,
PROFESSOR OF HISTORY

One of the older resident priests at Holy Cross taught history to most of us. I attended Father Lyons class when many of our classes were still being held at Holy Cross House, not at the new Butler Building. I don't recall much that was taught. I think Father knew History wasn't the most exciting subject for some of us.

When he mentioned the great navigators and explorers of the pre and post Columbus period, he frequently raised his voice and with a dramatic flourish, much like a stage actor setting a scene, would enliven his lectures.

"Sniff the sea breezes with Ferdinand Magellan, as he and his five ships sail across the Pacific!" or, "Join the Canadian explorer, Louis Joliet, as he explores the Great Lakes and discovers the Mississippi River!"

Father Lyons was of average, perhaps even small build, white haired and under six feet tall. A dedicated walker, he carried a walking stick, sometimes a cane. While playing football or baseball on the senior playing field, we often saw Father walking out St. Mary's Road. At other times he'd take a quick stroll around St. Joe Lake, or be seen walking quickly up from the Holy Cross entrance, returning from a jaunt on Notre Dame's main campus.

One day Father returned to Holy Cross from the direction of Moreau Seminary, walking quickly past the new Butler Building. It was a crisp fall day and I noticed steam when he exhaled, indicating to me that he'd most likely completed one of his hikes.

As he approached, he stopped for a moment to tie his shoe, lowering his knee to the ground. Through his black slacks, I noticed the outline of large, developed leg muscles and realized how powerfully built he was. He walked by, nodded and smiled to us as he often did, and entered Holy Cross through the senior rec room door.

It was about mid semester when I realized Father raised his voice and spoke in flowery prose to awaken a classmate who was nodding off. I was one of them.

FATHER DEAN O'DONNELL
and English Class

Father Dean O'Donnell—we called him "Father O'D"-- taught English and resided at Holy Cross year 'round. His teaching style was low-key, and laid back.

Upon his arrival at English class, you could count on a cheerful "Hello folks," Father's daily greeting. At every class I attended, Father appeared upbeat. He lit up the room with his presence.

Frequently, Father selected class essays that he read out loud, and then asked the class for constructive criticism. I remember once when my turn came up. The essay described Conroy's Funeral Home, back in my home town near Pittsburgh. I had used the word "wainscoting" to describe the wood paneling in the funeral home. Apparently, over the years, between Pittsburgh and the mid-west, the term had been lost. No one seemed to know what wainscoting was, and a few members of the class finally admitted they thought the essay was copied. The comments came as a shock to Father O'D, and particularly to me. These were my close buddies for three years. What had I done to deserve the comment?

Father quickly corrected the naysayers, explaining that he had been reading my essays for awhile and this was definitely my work. I felt proud. He further assured the class there were many of my old mistakes appearing in the essay. I have seldom felt my ego inflated and deflated so quickly.

In our junior year, Father O'D had everyone memorize two of several passages he had selected from Shakespeare's writing. To this day I can recall most of Marullus's speech,
"You rocks, you stones,
you worse than senseless things…"
and Macbeth's,
"Tomorrow, and tomorrow and tomorrow,
Creeps in it's petty pace from day to day…"
On the other hand we had to read Milton's "Paradise Lost" and "Paradise Regained." Although I had a genuine interest in the readings, I don't recall a single passage from the book.

Father O'D had a sneaky way of teaching writing. In our junior year he would read from Poe and Twain. In our senior year, he began reading John Steinbeck's "The Red Pony," spreading the chapters over several weeks. It was Father O'D's way of saying, "listen carefully to these people's writing. Anyone can write well if they hear how good writers write."

Father's technique for grading composition was supportive of the student's efforts. He stated on the student's paper whether he thought the writing was strong or weak, and graded a marginal paper with two grades: "This is a C or B." He used praise not criticism to inspire better writing.

In mid-September 1953, while recovering from a knee injury suffered during the Junior-Senior football game, I was transferred from the Notre Dame Infirmary to St. Joseph's Hospital to have the knee drained.

I decided to design a post card on a piece of paper—even drew a two-cent stamp on the front right corner--and addressed it to his room, *"Father O'D, Headquarters, Sleepy Hollow."* My short note described the exciting moment at St. Joseph Hospital, when a Dr. Bodner and his nurse injected the knee with pontocaine to deaden the nerves, then withdrew several needles full (I said "needle fulls") of blood near the knee cap. I was surprised when Father O'D graded the paper post card: *"A or B"*, and returned it.

Since our sophomore year, several of us had sung at daily Masses celebrated by resident priests, held in rooms outside the chapel. Often, Skinner and I sang at Fr O'D's Mass. Father's singing became an unusual trill on high notes, giving new meaning to the word "vibrato." This was natural in his singing voice, not an affected or conscious effort on Father's part. We thought he lent beauty to the Mass with his vocal gift. I wished later that someone had recorded his singing . Father O'D would have made an impressive addition to the tenor section of our 4-part a cappella choir.

Father O'D, a devout religious, would often pace outside Holy Cross House reading his Office. On warm days it wasn't unusual to see him in his swim suit, alone on the St. Mary's pier, reading.

In his subtle way, Father O'D left his mark on each of us. In English class he provided a daily respite from the demands of our other classes.

Father John VanWolvlear

THE UNOFFICIAL FOOTBALL KICKING CONTEST

Father's punt rose well above the mature trees that skirted the junior playing field. The football spiraled upward at a 45 degree angle. At its apex, the ball appeared to level out, parallel to the ground, float momentarily, then, its trajectory spent, plummet to the ground at the far end of the junior field, near St. Mary's Road.

PREP SCHOOL DAYS The Seminary at the University of Notre Dame

Father VanWolvlear--we called him Father Van--was a tall man, powerfully built through the shoulders and upper chest. Whether maneuvering on the playing field, or on the tennis court (before departing for the tennis courts, Father Van often commented: "I have a pastoral appointment at the court"), or simply walking down the main corridor at Holy Cross, Father Van's movements seemed more that of a cat's than of a large man.

His appearance, even as he aged, was undeniably that of an athlete. His persona is best described as that of a calm and empathetic priest who enjoyed his role as resident advisor, teacher and confessor at Holy Cross.

Father picked up another football repeating perfectly his earlier kick, then another, and another. Punting a football was an occasional after dinner sport for Father Van. Usually one or two of the resident priests and a covey of students followed him down to the junior playing field. We would fan out at the far end of the field, hoping to retrieve and return footballs quickly enough for Father to continue repeating his inspiring kicks.

Father's punting exercise often happened immediately after dinner on warm, summer evenings. Normally, Father would be wearing his cassock. He'd hitch up one end and tuck it in his belt. His street shoes and dark slacks didn't impede him in any way. Every punt was a perfectly executed spiral, each football landing in a predictable pattern at the other end of the junior field.

Ed Doyle, a junior from Chicago, had a medium build. He may have weighed as much as 160 pounds; certainly no more. Doyle was a good athlete. He also had strong endurance, proven when he almost beat my brother, Norm, a senior, in a race up Tower Hill at Lake Michigan.

Doyle had just arrived on the field from the refectory. Father Van had kicked his final punt, watching it land while talking to Father O'D. As they turned to advance up the small rise of grass toward Holy Cross, the solid sound of a well kicked football made both priests turn. The ball spiraled upward, flattened at its zenith and plunged to the ground. Both priests were smiling and talking quietly to each other. Father Van finally said, "Mister Doyle, can you do that again?"

Doyle again executed a perfect spiral punt across the field toward St. Joe House. "Father, can you match that one?" Doyle derided, smiling.

"Mister Doyle must have eaten his Wheaties this morning. That was a very nice punt. Was it one of those smaller footballs or regulation size?"

Doyle laughed, grabbed one of the balls retrieved for Father Van and booted another punt as beautiful as the last.

Maybe Doyle realized he was a little off base challenging Father one-on-one. He quickly replied, "I'm working on distance, Father. Maybe some day I'll kick one as far as you."

"You're doing just fine, Mister Doyle. Keep up the good work and I'll see you the next time."

Doyle remained on the field kicking several perfect spirals, until the two priests disappeared into the building. With each of Doyle's punts, Fathers Van and O'D glanced back to watch the spiraling ball arch upward and land at the far end of the junior field, near St. Mary's Road.

LOCKER ROOM INVASION

It happened in the early fall of our junior year. Dinner had been served and many of us had completed our meals. A sophomore appeared in the doorway of the refectory obviously frightened, yelling that a man was in the freshman locker room. About a dozen seniors, including Speltz and Algeo, raced from the refectory.

It wasn't long before they returned, discussing the search for the man, and the fact that he'd been confronted on St. Mary's Road, near the outdoor Stations of the Cross. The man, probably a war veteran living on the road—they called them hobos--apologized profusely, his pants suddenly appearing wet. All he wanted to do was find food, he explained.

The group felt sorry for him, so a few of them marched him around to the kitchen entrance, asking Sister Zacharia if she could provide the man a sandwich and something to drink. Because there had been another recent locker room "invasion" and items were missing, campus security was called.

The man ate his meal out by the spud house not realizing until security arrived that he was going to be detained.

Algeo said the man was so frightened he doubted he would ever come near Holy Cross again.

ROGER SOWALA

Every morning at breakfast, Rog Sowala, our table head, followed the same routine. First he grabbed a cereal bowl from the stack on the table. "Grabbed" is the proper word here because Sowala had large palms and long fingers that could easily grasp a basketball one handed, or hide a football for a later pass to a down-field receiver. So once his hand reached for a bowl, there was little doubt, he owned it.

He would tear open several small boxes of cereal, dump them in the bowl and pour milk over the cereal. All nine of us tablemates would quietly await his next move. His reach for the sugar.

The sugar container, glass restaurant style, held at least a cup and a half of sugar and had a metal top with a pour spout. Sowala swept the bottle off the table, and held it over his cereal for what seemed like 30 seconds. If the sugar came in a bowl, which it often did, it didn't bother Sowala. He heaped teaspoon after teaspoon of sugar into the cereal bowl, until the cereal disappeared and only the white mountain of sugar topping could be seen. The rest of the table had to use sugar from another bowl at the far end of the table, or quietly pirate sugar from other tables.

Sowala did something that left a lasting impression. Simultaneously he carried on a conversation with one person, laughed at the joke of another, and debated some unimportant issue of the day, all while devouring coffee, toast, and cereal.

Sowala was a bright and capable student, far beyond some of us. He not only excelled in the classroom, but on the playing field. And most importantly, the priests and brothers at Holy Cross liked and respected him.

Yet, I can say, without a qualm of conscience, that in spite of his many wonderful attributes, Sowala had failings. For example, he couldn't beat John Butler or Tom Norris every time they played against each other at table tennis or on the shuffle board, even though he seemed to effortlessly dominate these two activities during day and evening rec-room breaks. Occasionally he lost a football game, even though he had the best team at Holy Cross, me included. And he needed the help of several other classmates to soundly beat St. Joe's, a highly ranked Indiana High School basketball team.

Sowala had a knack for consistently giving a good hair cut. Ron Vogel also cut hair, as did John Coyne who contributed for a short time. All three had a knack for cutting hair. But, for selfish reasons, I went to Sowala. I knew I could rely on his extroverted nature to hear many of the jokes, stories and most of the rumors circulating around Holy Cross.

I was Holy Cross steam man, living in a third floor room, away from fellow classmates. Sowala took it upon himself to keep me informed. For instance, he mentioned that Joe Schott, from Indianapolis, was caught late one evening stealing peanut butter from the food pantry, near the Sister's quarters. Sowala predicted that Schott would be expelled. He was.

There's one other thing about Sowala that probably exasperated some of us. He worked tirelessly in the foreign missions office, doing correspondence and collecting stamps off response envelopes, when most of us were still in study hall, or in our rooms cramming for the next day's classes.

God, how we loved and admired that guy.

...SENIOR YEAR...

SIXTEEN-INCH BALL:
PASSING A DANGEROUS SUMMER'S EVE

Along with the junior class, we seniors arrived at Holy Cross two weeks early to prepare the house for the new freshman arrivals and the sophomores who had successfully made it through the tough first year of studies, sports, silences and homesickness.

In the evenings it was not unusual to get a group together to play sixteen inch ball, a Midwestern softball tradition. The ball is a third larger than the traditional 12 inch softball. The playing field is a third smaller than a baseball field.

Forget a glove. Softball or baseball gloves are unable to easily handle the larger sized ball, though pitchers sometimes wear them. It's a bare handed, fast moving game. Base paths are reduced to two-thirds of the 90 feet required in regulation baseball, and the pitcher's mound -to-home plate distance is reduced accordingly.

We had a great game going. For a pitcher we had Father Fiedler, lobbing a slow pitched ball to the batter. Being experienced hard ball batters the opposing team swung and missed the ball repeatedly, their reaction time not in sync with slow pitch nor the arc of the ball.

PREP SCHOOL DAYS The Seminary at the University of Notre Dame

Father Fiedler had an advantage that the opposing pitcher, Carl Bufalini, lacked. Father possessed very large, strong hands, easily able to grasp the oversized ball and control the pitch. Father quickly struck out three batters and we came in from the field to bat.

Our team had a tall, thin gentleman visiting from Old College, the seminary for College students, across Saint Mary's Lake. I don't recall his name, but he reminded more than one of us of the character, Ichabod Crane, in the movie cartoon, "The Headless Horseman." He was tall and had long, thin arms sticking out of an untucked tee shirt. His batter's stance was to stand a few feet back from the plate and stoop over, an easy target for Bufalini.

Bufalini had an unusual delivery. He'd stand perfectly erect, his 240 pound, 6 foot frame dominating the mound. In the late day sun, his shadow reached tenaciously toward homeplate. He stooped quickly and with an upward motion delivered the ball in a high arc. He then immediately reassumed an erect position. Two of our batters, used to fast-pitch baseball, had already struck out.

I will never forget Crane (sorry for the name change) coming up to the plate, looking somewhat uncoordinated, due mostly to his lanky build. Bufalini made his delivery. Quicker then anyone could react, Crane connected with the ball, a line drive directly at Bufalini. When the bat connected it mimicked the crack of a bat meeting a baseball, a loud thwack!

Two years of sports had made Bufalini a good athlete. His hands' reflex action caught the ball just as it hit his solar plexus. A small puff of smoke arose from the ball. Bufalini stood petrified on the mound, his breath gone and unable to move or respond in any way. The ball rolled out of his hands and fell to the ground. At first we thought the stitching on the ball dissolved, and the leather cover had fallen to the ground, but it was the ball.

Not realizing that Bufalini was hurt, we yelled at Crane to run the bases. Crane dropped his bat and ran, leaping around the short base path, looking more like a malnourished gazelle than a man.

According to Father Brinker, Father Fiedler hurried to the mound, followed by Fathers Banas and Vanwolvlear. The priests lowered Bufalini to the ground. Bufalini came around, recovering somewhat from Mr. Crane's assault, and wanted to continue pitching. After we realized what had happened to Bufalini, the game lost some of its intensity. No one remembers the score or who won.

PREP SCHOOL DAYS The Seminary at the University of Notre Dame

Part of the Holy Cross line-up
Back Row: Dick Kovalik, Don Kaiser, Jon Lullo, Jim Keating
Front Row: Rog Sowala, Cy Speltz, Mike Wilsey, Mike Gelven, Ed Whelan

HOCKEY, FOOTBALL, BASKETBALL and BASEBALL

Holy Cross is a seminary for future priests. Priests are educated men of honor, admired for their priest-like qualities of love and forgiveness... except on the playing field. The priests at Holy Cross played as hard at sports as any dedicated sports pro. We learned to play fair--the Golden Rule in sports--or else--but to play hard.

Hockey...My closest sibling, Norm, played ice hockey for several seasons on the rough ice of St. Mary's Lake.

Following his novitiate year—I'm sure he played some hockey there, in Bennington, Vermont as well--he played hockey at Stonehill College in North Easton, Massachusetts. Later, I heard a rumor that interest was expressed in recruiting Norm for one of the Canadian hockey teams.

I recall a winter in 1958, when I was on Christmas leave from the Navy and returned to Pittsburgh. Norm was attending Duquesne University.

One evening we drove out to Swan Lake, near the Pittsburgh Airport. People were attempting to ice skate but there was a local team of young hockey players dominating the ice. Norm grabbed a hockey stick out of the car trunk, put on a pair of ice skates, and skated over to the team of high school hockey players to ask if they wanted to challenge him to a one point game. They snickered among themselves and shot him the puck. He pushed the puck back to them and said, "Whoever makes a point, first. If I do you clear the ice for the other skaters." A few of them were laughing and circling the puck. As soon as one of the team took the puck and began a drive, Norm neatly took it away from him, drove through their defense to the other end of the lake, and flipped the puck off the ice onto the grass. He offered to do it again, but they backed off. I was surprised, but not as surprised as the other five hockey players. And Norm was wearing an old pair of figure skates.

Zero Degrees Fahrenheit-- and Holding... As a side comment on the cold weather in Northern Indiana, at the beginning of a beautiful sunny day, there was an announcement that the temperature was zero degrees. I had not experienced a zero degree cold. I couldn't imagine the temperature being that cold in the bright sunlight.

PREP SCHOOL DAYS The Seminary at the University of Notre Dame

It was after completing my obedience in the senior rec room—straightening out chairs, arranging each deck of cards in the shape of a gambler's rose on the half dozen tables—and a few minutes before the day's classes were to begin next door at the Butler Building that I decided to test the outside air in my tee-shirt and slacks. Not a breeze stirred as I stepped off the stairs into the outside air. My intention was to walk toward the front of Holy Cross and re-enter the building at the center doors on the far side of the junior rec room, no more than a 30 second walk, then proceed upstairs to my room to dress for classes.

Several steps into my walk, the wind stirred up old leaves in the grass above the junior playing field, creating a wind dervish that sped across the walkway toward the junior rec room. Experiencing the ice cold draft, I reversed my direction and headed back toward the senior rec room entrance only to encounter a group of my classmates, dressed in coats and scarves, exiting the building, headed toward our first class at the Butler Building.

With arms crossed and a sick bravado painted on my face, I calmly watched Sowala, Wood, Callahan, and several others pass me as I patiently awaited my chance to enter through the door and into the warm inside.

Father O'D appeared, following behind the crowd, a long, knitted white scarf tied loosely around his neck. Father jumped the few steps to the ground, stopped for a moment, looked me up and down sadly, and commented, "My goodness, you must be cold." He then walked quickly toward the Butler Building to catch up to the group. I felt a chill for the rest of that long class day.

Football... A Holy Cross example of not turning the other cheek comes to mind. A junior heavies football team was playing a tense game against a senior heavies team. We juniors were ahead by a touchdown, and had possession of the ball. Rog Sowala, our quarterback, called a quick huddle and a quick center. Sowala handed the ball off to Duane Boudreaux, a sophomore from Oklahoma.

Boudreaux a strong country boy, rumbled down the field like a young bull. A senior, Ray "Big Ray" Zaradnik, saw the opportunity to blind-side Boudreaux, and, without additional thought, nailed him.

The ball dislodged from Boudreaux's meaty hands and bounced into a senior's arms. We tagged the senior almost immediately, but the damage had been done. The ball was in the possession of the senior team.

Boudreaux was unhurt, rolling over, raising more dust than two people. He got slowly to his feet and sauntered over to the huddle.

We knew what was going on in Boudreaux's mind, and were sure Zahradnik knew what Boudreaux would be up to. Following the snap of the ball, Boudreaux's block hit Zahradnik's 180 pounds and flipped him. Zahradnik spun in the air and landed hard on his side.

Too proud to admit hurt, Zahradnik, dazed, limped and stumbled to his team huddle. Any football referee would have penalized both individuals for their unsportsmanlike conduct. But Boudreaux was quietly heralded as a hero. Sooner or later the lesson had to be taught to Zahradnik.

Notre Dame Home Games...The excitement felt in our Holy Cross group , invited to attend Notre Dame home football games, particularly during the 1953 and 1954 winning seasons, is an unforgettable memory. We were most likely the only attendees appearing in black suits, white shirts, black ties, and black hats—our Holy Cross Seminary formal wear. Fortunately, fall days in northern Indiana are chilly, so most of us wore overcoats over our suits.

Typically we had seating in the upper rows of Notre Dame Stadium. Several of us had Notre Dame team programs, and some others had binoculars, hardly needed, since we already knew our favorite players and their positions. The two history making seasons are a credit to two great coaches and their dedicated and talented players. In 1953 Coach Frank Leahy had a 9 – 0 – 1 season and in 1954 Coach Terry Brennan had a 9 – 1 season. There were all-time great players like quarterback, Ralph Guglielmi, and halfback Johnny Lattner. Paul Hornung, the "Golden Boy" could play halfback, fullback and quarterback with equal skill. He was a natural. Joe Schott, a high school coach all his life, would comment later that Paul Hornung was so quick and agile on the field, few people realized he was six-foot-two inches tall and 215 pounds..

We were most fortunate to be a small part of the all male Notre Dame campus of the 1950's. Frequently, football players would walk from the main campus and up St. Mary's road to the women's college. Both of Holy Cross's junior and senior fields bordered the road. If we were playing a football game, the players would often stop and participate, throwing a few passes, or just talking football with us.

Basketball... During our sophomore year, we played basketball on an outdoor half court, located about a hundred yards west of Holy Cross, near St. Mary's Lake.

Andrew Stevans

For our junior and senior years, basketball was played on a full court, in the new Butler Building, constructed across the north foot path from Holy Cross House. The building had a long entrance corridor with classrooms on either side. At the far end, through swinging doors, we had an enclosed handball court to the left, and the basketball court to the right.

What a boon for the star, house-team. The court was regulation size and quality, and had enough room for a bleacher section near the front.

By our senior year, there were few of us remaining, with a class of only 24. Fortunately, the junior class had one or two basketball up-and-comers, and together, juniors and seniors practiced daily, filtering out the best players for each position, and perfecting a zone defense.

The previous year, St Joe High School, located a short distance from Notre Dame, had a crack basketball team with a high ranking in Indiana. Toward spring of our senior year, someone, I believe it was Father Simmons, decided to invite St. Joe's team over to Holy Cross to play our short staffed team.

We had a strong first team consisting of John Butler, Bill Klouda, Tom Norris, Joe Schott and Rog Sowala. Holy Cross had only four of a normal five substitutes on the bench. There was John Berry, who suffered an eye injury, and couldn't play. That left Jim Keating, Jerry Wood, Jon Lullo, and Jim Callahan.

Holy Cross was taken off guard when St. Joe arrived with a team taller than the Holy Cross team, a full contingent of substitutes and a squad of attractive, uniformed cheer leaders.

The game moved fast. Holy Cross was able to hold its own during the first half. During the second half an earlier emphasis on zone-play started to reap rewards. John Butler, Tom Norris and Rog Sowala had practiced a passing game that included multiple hand offs near the basket. During the middle of the second half, Holy Cross took the lead. We never lost it, and soon dominated the game. The final score of 86 to 66 was elating to say the least. There were few times when I experienced Holy Cross players, coaches and attendees carrying on to the point of shouting and reveling in the win over a much larger school that should have easily won the game.

Sowala and Butler each scored 20 points, Schott 16 points. The remaining 30 points were shared between Klouda and Norris.

Holy Cross's basketball team was formidable, but not unbeatable. We played the Notre Dame freshman team. We lost. And an intramural basketball team, mostly football players (Sam Palumbo, Paul Hornung, and several others) and beat them badly.

Baseball... In the spring of our Junior year, several of the house priests, all experienced sportsmen, began putting together a Holy Cross House baseball team. We met daily, and began a priest-directed series of practices geared toward building an unbeatable batting and fielding capability.

Father Bill Brinker, backed by Fr Joseph "Harry" Fiedler coached each position, providing us the expertise of their many years of playing experience. I played third base. Under both priests' trained and watchful eye, I fielded grounders and learned how to throw to first base without hesitation, by stepping forward and spinning off my left foot. After satisfying our coaches that we were the best we could ever be, our House team acquired Notre Dame baseball uniforms. The intense practices had paid off with easy wins against other Holy Cross teams.

In an initial game, we were invited to play Moreau Seminary, the college equivalent of Holy Cross. It was a cold May day, with snow flurries in the air. We looked impressive in our Notre Dame uniforms. Holy Cross offered some strong competition, but lost the game to Moreau. It was chalked up as a loss to an older and more experienced team.

Sacred Heart Preparatory Seminary in Donaldson Indiana had a baseball team. We were invited to Sacred Heart for a game. It was late in the spring and this game would be our last before the summer break.

After an hour bus ride down the Liberty Highway, Holy Cross arrived at Sacred Heart. Upon disembarking from the bus, it was obvious to everyone where we were from. The words "Notre Dame" were emblazoned across the fronts of our uniforms.

The opposing Sacred Heart team appeared in street clothes. Their pitcher was nondescript, on the lanky side, and appeared a bit slow during his warm up. Then the game began.

To this day, I can remember the "WOP!" of the delivery as each fast ball hit the catcher's mitt.

"You're out!" resounded after each Holy Cross player went through the at-plate exercise. It didn't matter the batting order, or the substitutes, or the coaches' strategy. We simply couldn't hit off this Sacred Heart pitcher. His ability to sustain a fast ball delivery for many innings was a wake-up call for our team.

Cy Speltz, our experienced pitcher, had a consistent delivery that had won Holy Cross many games. We suffered through hit after hit from the Sacred Heart batters.

During one of the later innings, with Holy Cross at bat and two out, I managed to connect with the ball. It was a solid line drive down the third base line almost hitting Sacred Heart's third baseman. The ball continued into left field. I made it to first base or second with Keating advancing to third after stealing second earlier. It didn't really matter. We struck out again.

The Holy Cross/Notre Dame uniforms no longer looked as new as they had just a short time earlier. I remember Keating's looking like he had slid into all four bases on his stomach.

After hitting the line drive, I favored my right hand for the remainder of the game. Why the bat didn't shatter on impact, I can't explain. I felt its vibration up both arms. We lost that game--big time.

(Courtesy of Bill and Mary Lou Klouda)
Skating on St. Mary's Lake following a hockey game

SR. LIFE SAVING, SWIMMING – and WADING

Our group had several strong swimmers. In fact, early in our senior year, a dozen of us attended the Senior Life Saving course at Notre Dame's Rockne Hall, located on the south side of St. Mary's Lake, directly opposite Holy Cross. The life guard instructor at Rockne Hall was muscular, built like a football player. This contradicted his philosophy on swimming.

During one of the earlier classes we were split into two teams to swim relays. I experienced difficulty maintaining swimming speed. The instructor commented that swimming uses long muscles of the body most efficiently, similar to the type muscles developed playing basketball. He explained that bunched muscles--I was selected for his example--were a necessary ingredient for football, but these heavier muscles would not serve us well in life saving, since they would tire the swimmer by expending energy merely to remain afloat. He emphasized that the heavier muscles could also contribute to more body and leg cramps. From then on I felt my days were numbered in the Senior Life Saving course.

One of our initial assignments was to swim the length of the pool a dozen times. We could use any stroke: freestyle, back stroke, side or breast stroke, even a doggie paddle, but we had to complete 12 laps of the pool. I suffered a leg cramp but was able to complete the laps. In later sessions we each had to retrieve a large solid rubber brick from the bottom of the deepest part of the pole. The instructor was excellent. His teaching method was to build on earlier classes. We reached a point where we were actually saving a drowning victim (fellow classmate). We were shown how to enter the water quickly by jumping into the water feet first while simultaneously executing a scissor-kick to remain on the water's surface and maintain visual contact with the victim. Upon approaching the victim we were taught to dive under water to keep the drowning victim from grabbing us. We would then turn the victim away from us and climb up his body from behind. By using the cross-chest carry we'd bring him safely to the side of the pool. As a final test, we each had to save the instructor, who fought us and attempted to drag us under.

Everyone in the group successfully passed the difficult course and received a Red Cross, Senior Life Saving card and a three-inch round patch having the Red Cross in the center and yellow words against a blue background around the circumference stating "Senior Life Saving."

Swimming... At Holy Cross, swimming in St. Mary's lake required a buddy system, where two swimmers agreed to watch out for each other. After our group passed Senior Life Saving, we were asked to keep a watchful eye when there were Holy Cross swimmers using the St. Mary's pier. On trips to Tower Hill, the same buddy system was used, but we patrolled the Lake Michigan beach, keeping an eye open for potential problems. Many in our small senior class wore "the patch."

A few years later, I was stationed in Newport Rhode Island with the U.S. Navy, a short drive from Stonehill

College. It was early summer and I decided to take advantage of an Instructor's Life Saving course offered at Jones Beach, nearby.

I arrived early, went to the beach house and changed into my swim suit, my Sr. Life Saving patch prominently displayed. No one had arrived for the first class, so I decided to walk the beach at the water's edge. A large wave hit shore. I stepped back too late. The bitter cold waters of the North Atlantic drenched me. I recalled how cold St. Mary's Lake was in early spring, when a few of us undertook cleaning up debris around the pier. We shook so badly from the cold we found it difficult to direct our bodies to our bathrobes hanging just a few feet from the pier. The North Atlantic's water was that cold.

Not easily dissuaded, I attempted one more entry into the water, diving into an incoming wave. I then returned to the beach house, toweled off, changed back into my street clothes and returned to the Newport Naval base.

Wading... On a Saturday morning in the late summer, a group of us juniors decided to hike out to Juday Creek. I hadn't left the seminary grounds during my sophomore year except to attend Notre Dame home games with classmates, or on Visiting Sundays to eat at the Notre Dame cafeteria with family.

Juday Creek, a meandering stream near Notre Dame, was a surprise. Its waters were no more than a few feet deep in most spots and crystal clear. I noticed no white water. Groundwater springs fed the Creek, allowing it to maintain its purity. Fish, particularly trout, appeared abundant in the slow moving stream. We noticed many minnows, dragonflies, water spiders and other aquatic insects. I was glad I came.

Of the group, I recall Sowala, Whelan, Wood, Lullo, Keating, Callahan, Wilsey and Gelven, I was the only one of the group who had not hiked Juday Creek. We walked the sandy bottom without fear of debris other than stones and submerged limbs and roots.

We enjoyed a pleasant late morning and early afternoon at Juday Creek, then hiked over to Pinhook Lake, behind St. Mary's Women's College, Notre Dame's sister college. The lake had what appeared to be an island 30 yards from shore. Later, I learned it was the inner land portion of the horseshoe shaped lake—thus the name "Pinhook."

One of our group, possibly Wilsey, decided to swim across to a submerged log, near shore. It was not a good decision. Wilsey easily swam across but developed a leg cramp, then a stomach cramp. He made it to the far shore, but was unable to swim back across to rejoin the group. Two of us finally decided to swim across and bring Wilsey back on the log. It worked.

The day ended too quickly.

FATHER BILL SIMMONS and GREEK CLASS
Για την τιμή και δόξα του Θεού
A.M.D.G

G reek 101 (first year), was taught in our senior year at Holy Cross, along with two additional languages: advanced Latin and advanced French. Although the four-year Holy Cross curriculum was classical, students were also required to take algebra, trigonometry, and physics. Additionally, many in the class took basic chemistry. I didn't, and later wished that I had. A basic chemistry course would have given me a definite leg-up during a semester at NAPS, the Navy Prep School for Naval Academy appointees.

Father Simmons knew his Greek. He was able to follow the Greek primer's examples with examples of his own, and often providing additional insights, enhancing what he said with elaborate Greek-looking scratches on the chalk board. According to Fr. Simmons, Greek would be relatively

PREP SCHOOL DAYS The Seminary at the University of Notre Dame

easy. He assured us the Greek language wasn't nearly as hard as Sanskrit, the Indian root language we'd begin to learn in our novitiate year.

I quickly realized that not only was the Greek alphabet a hurdle, but the pronunciation was well beyond my limited Western Pennsylvanian English dialect. I prayed hard for divine assistance, as hard as I did two years earlier during the geometry fiasco. It simply wasn't happening soon enough.

For several weeks into the semester, I struggled with Greek, mentioning my exasperation in weekly letters home. Finally, oldest brother, Jack, came to my rescue in the form of a "cheat sheet." Typical of older brothers, Jack expected nothing in return, nor did he want to be bothered with my expressions of gratitude.

But a small packet of 35 vocabulary cards, measuring two-inches by four-inches, arrived in an unmarked business envelope. Each card contained eight English words with their Greek translations on the opposite side. Included with the cards was a note-book containing the translations for each exercise in the Greek 101 primer.

Jack's gift was a God-send. Far beyond my abilities at Holy Innocents grade school, Jack had now demonstrated his scholarship at Holy Cross. During that year, Father Simmons was more than pleased with my translations, and probably made some margin of allowance for my poor showing on exams.

Over the years I misplaced the notebook of Greek 101 translations, possibly giving it to another struggling Greek scholar. Yet, for some reason lost to the ages, I still have the

English/Greek vocabulary cards with my name, along with "AMDG." (Latin: "For the Honor and Glory of God"), inscribed on the front card.

Later, I discovered that Jack's act of mercy was a duplication of an act of mercy shown him. The note book of Greek 101 translations was a pirated copy provided him while at Holy Cross. He swears that the 35 English-to-Greek vocabulary cards are his own.

Older brother, Jack, 1954

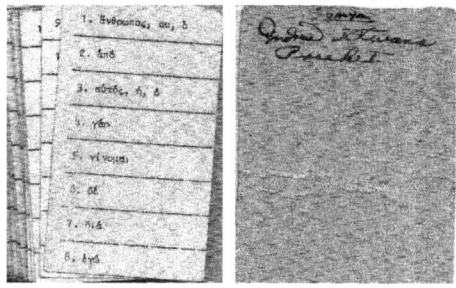

Roommates, Bell Ringing and Father Bill Brinker's Physics Class

Holy Cross Seniors had shared rooms on the second and third floors of the old building. Tom Norris and Jon Lullo shared a room directly across the hall from Andy Roering's and my (steam men's) room. Both of our rooms were located at the very end of the third floor hall looking out toward St. Mary's Lake, the Notre Dame Dome and Sacred Heart Church. I recall that Jim Glaza roomed with Jim Keating. Next to Glaza's room, Harry Krush and Jude McKusker shared a room near the top of the third floor steps, just above the entrance to the second floor chapel. From this vantage point, we could look down at the chapel entrance through a window-like opening on the landing between the second and third floors. Lee Skinner and Dave Gibson shared a room on the second floor, near the library. Krush, McKusker and Skinner were scholars, able to attend Notre Dame freshmen classes in their senior year. I secretly envied their abilities but decided early on not to bother them with my minutia, namely, Father Brinker's difficult physics assignments.

Each morning Tom Norris was responsible for awakening all students. He rang a hand-held brass bell. He would open the door to each of the 12 senior-resident rooms and ding the hand bell once saying (in Latin) "Benedicamus Domino"(Let us bless the Lord) to which we would respond "Deo Gratias" (Thanks be to God). Norris then quickly shut the door. I don't recall him hanging around to hear our response. He had 12 senior rooms to awaken on the third floor.

He then had to walk to the second floor, across a windowed atrium to the new building to awaken the Freshmen, Sophomore, and Juniors located in second and third floor dorms.

Andy Roering and I wondered if Norris dinged the bell to awaken Jon Lullo, his roommate across the hall. If so, we never heard the ding. And yet we heard the bell at each room on down the third floor hall. Roering decided that Lullo got a break to sleep in for another 10 minutes, or at least until Norris completed his rounds. I decided that the "Piggies clique" comprised of Norris, Lullo and Vogel, all from Chicago, was alive and well, and Lullo got up at his own speed. Of course, this was conjecture...

I often had tall hurdles to jump when it came to solving physics problems. I recall some frustration with the algebraic equations for converting Fahrenheit to Centigrade and Centigrade to Fahrenheit.

Jon Lullo exited his room and was moving fast when I asked if he had solved the previous day's physics assignment. We were on a grand silence until breakfast, but I was feeling a growing desperation. Lullo quickly looked at my open physics book and quickly scanned the assignment.

"Ah, no. Sorry. I'm going to work on that later this morning." Lullo continued at his quick pace down the hall.

I had always classified both Lullo and Gibson as math whizzes. Physics' algebraic equations should have been a snap for either of them. On the other hand, due to poor study habits, I had barely passed first year algebra at St. James, back in Pittsburgh. I could only blame myself. I stood in the hall for a moment, half hoping that Lullo would turn and say,

"Oh, yeah. I remember now..."

It didn't happen.

I waited for Norris to return from bell ringing to ask his help in solving the problem. I finally concluded that he had gone directly to chapel. I too attended chapel and, while I was kneeling during the Mass, I was able to scratch possible solutions on the top railing of the chapel seat in front of me. I learned during a difficult sophomore Geometry class that the markings easily erased. I started over many times.

It then occurred to me that the steam room had a outdoor thermometer that provided both Fahrenheit and Centigrade readings at any given temperature. Following chapel and breakfast, I took the physics book to the steam room, fed coal to satisfy the hungry furnace, then spent the next 30 minutes sitting on the cold basement steam-room steps, substituting values in the equation until the answers matched the outdoor thermometer readings. For a brief period of time, I felt I was a tiny bit ahead of the ball in Father Brinker's Physics class.

Andrew Stevans

HOMICIDE DETECTIVE

Heavy set and quick witted, with a no-nonsense quality to his stage persona, Gerry Matheny, from Indianapolis, was a natural for the part of Detective O'Reilly. Matheny dominated the stage in the unusual murder mystery, penned by several of us seniors. I recall Jim Keating, Jim Callahan, and Jim Glaza all contributed time and effort to the play. Others helped with the stage setting, lighting and direction.

After some basic inquiry among the writers, no one seemed to remember this one-act play. I remember only that the plot was easy to follow...

Joe Smith had been missing for several days. He turned up dead. A world traveler, Mr. Smith was aware of the risks in his chosen profession as a bird smuggler.

Detective O'Reilly was not one to be fooled easily. Long before Inspector Clouseau and the Pink Panther series, Detective O'Reilly's "interrogation speak" closely followed a Clouseau logic.

"Don't you agree; he who don't know nothing, must know something?" or

"There's a time to laugh and a time not to laugh. This is not one of them."

Detective O'Reilly's cunning and wordsmithing created fear and awe among the criminal element—according to Detective O'Reilly.

PREP SCHOOL DAYS The Seminary at the University of Notre Dame

The play was considered a hit at Holy Cross. Unfortunately, over the years the play was misplaced, or else stored away in the archives, somewhere on the Notre Dame grounds.

I'm sure the Notre Dame archives and Province Archives Center are far more organized than, for example, the Pentagon archives. And I hope that soon someone discovers this memorable one-act play that gave a kind of immortality to Gerry.

(Courtesy of Jim Callahan)
**Detective Gerry Matheny and Special Agent James Callahan
Ready to serve at the drop of a hat—er, suitcase, 1955**

Andrew Stevans

HALLOWEEN: REFECTORY

The idea came to us during October, following a 4-part a cappella practice in the movie hall, "The Cave," located beneath the dining hall (refectory). Why couldn't we create an October scene in the refectory for the dinner meal on Halloween?

Later, a few of our classmates came up with the idea of driving a truck out to St. Joe farm to pick up some dried corn stalks. We would place several shocks of corn (a half dozen stalks tied together) along the main isle of the refectory. Someone suggested there should be something at the entrance to the refectory a little more unsettling than corn shocks, maybe a corn stalk scarecrow dressed in dungarees, an old plaid shirt and a hat. That suggestion brought immediate agreement. Now, the plan had to obtain approval from the Holy Cross superior, Father Riley.

The following week, Father Riley gave the idea the go-ahead. What we didn't initially disclose to Father was an additional plan for that evening; something that would take the entire house off guard—a voice from the grave.

The week before Halloween, a group of us obtained an old truck from Herman, the groundskeeper. Gelven drove. Several of us, including Gibson, Sowala, Norris, Lullo, Callahan and Wood jumped in the back of the truck for the trip out to St. Joe farm.

Our idea of "harvesting" corn stalks was simple enough. We grabbed a dry stalk, pulled it out of the ground and chopped off the root. After collecting several dozen, we returned to Holy Cross and stored the stalks temporarily in the spud house, a separate building near the kitchen.

The following day, we asked Klouda if he could reach the ceiling with a mop from "the Cave" beneath the refectory. He did so easily. We then transferred the speaker, used for readings during the meal, from the refectory to a speaker plug-in on the stage in the Cave, below. Our plan was almost complete.

The day before Halloween, Zahradnik, Callahan and I drove into South Bend to a JC Murphy's store. Murphy's had a hardware department and electrical supplies. For the refectory event, Father Riley approved and financed an extension cord, a circuit breaker and a double socket to hold two 4 watt round bulbs for the scarecrow's eyes. This would finalize the refectory plan.

During the afternoon of Halloween, a group of us dressed up the refectory with a half-dozen corn stalk shocks, and several pumpkins donated by Sister Zacharia. We hollowed out and cut faces into each pumpkin. Candles were inserted and placed in the refectory windows—on the outside. Greeting each arrival at the entrance to the refectory was the largest scarecrow we could make, sitting in a chair, fully dressed with blinking, white eyes behind a Paper Mache mask. Lighting was subdued.

Jim Callahan described the next decorating scene (scheme) perfectly. Dick "Lord" Cavanaugh was asked to be a corpse and was invited to view a nicely decorated coffin some of the group had constructed. To everyone's dismay, Cavanaugh entered wholeheartedly into the corpse-in-the-coffin idea.

The location of the coffin was crucial. When exiting the refectory there were five or six steps down to a darkened landing, and to the left of the landing, a flight of stairs descending into the basement of the old building that housed a workshop and the junior locker room--and a coffin. The coffin had been constructed in the workshop then dragged to the bottom of the steps. In order to view Cavanaugh and his casket, priests and students looked down the steps from the landing to the refectory, above.

Mr. Cavanaugh dressed up for the event in his black suit, white shirt and tie, and was laid out in the coffin, his face whitened with flour and make-up to give a corpse-like appearance. A light placed above and somewhat behind Cavanaugh's head, shadowed his eyes.

Cavanaugh looked as dead as any corpse. Klouda and I retreated to the cave, below the refectory.

Soon, the student body and priests could be heard entering the refectory, above. There was the pause and a mixture of comments and laughter about the coffin scene. We heard the scrap of chairs, above, as everyone prepared for the blessing and dinner.

"Benedicite," Father Riley began the Latin before-meal blessing.

All was quiet as servers began the delivery of food and drink to the tables. This was the perfect moment to begin Edgar Allen Poe's "The Telltale heart..." Skinner began playing a death dirge on the piano as the murderer explains that he's not mad at all. He spoke of the old man with the evil blue eyes. Toward the end of the brief story, the insane murderer hears the heartbeat from under the floor where he had buried the old man's body. Klouda began his thumping with the mop, against the ceiling, *"THUMP, thump; THUMP,*

thump" proceeding from the stage to the front of the refectory above. He slowly let the thumping fade as the insane killer confesses to the murder.

More than one student or priest inquired about the lectern having no reader, yet the voice came from the area of the lectern. Father Riley, who, at the last minute, was in on the prank, smiled and winked at us but was dismissive of the entire event.

Andrew Stevans

READER, PRIEST WAITER
HERMAN'S WORK SHOP

Father Riley, the Holy Cross superior, approached me to ask if I would read from a designated text to the student body during lunch each day. The "refectory reader" obedience had been assigned during Advent and Lent in order to maintain silence in the refectory while eating.

I enjoyed this vote of confidence. When students and priests entered to eat lunch, I was already at the reading lectern, at the far end of the refectory. The readings had a religious bent that reminded me of Fulton Oursler's book, "Modern Parables." It was an easy book to read. I had read one parable each day during my sophomore year at Holy Cross. This should be a piece of cake.

Unfortunately, Father Riley became my nemesis, "How do you pronounce that word?" I'd re-read the sentence. He would respond, "No, it's reminiscences, not reminisces."

This went on during each day of the reading. Constructive criticism, I'd say to myself.

"No, it's alternative, not alternate." "No, it's illusion, not allusion." "No, it's enormity; there's no such word as anormity." It went on, often several times during a single reading.

My confidence was waning, but I didn't let on. I consoled myself with the thought that, after the lunch crowd left the refectory, I could join the waiters at the waiters table and eat a leisurely lunch—without having to observe the silence.

Maybe my readings did impress Father Riley. Shortly after the reading assignment I had a new assignment. I became a priest-waiter, a three-times-a-day obedience.

There were always two designated priest waiters. Cy Speltz was the other waiter and a veteran, able to show me how to arrange place settings for the priests. On the fresh linen table cloth, each place setting had a large dinner plate and a bread plate with a folded linen napkin placed on top. A large fork and the smaller salad fork were placed to the left of the plate, two case knives to the right, a teaspoon, soup spoon and butter knife above the plate, a coffee cup and saucer to the right, and a filled water glass to the left. Three times each day, Cy and I set up for 25 priests and visitors.

On my first day as priest waiter, I took an empty coffee cup from Father Van's hand and refilled it; another time I filled Father Riley's coffee cup, as it set on the table. Father Riley gave Cy a look that said, "fix it." Cy advised me to reach over a priest's shoulder only after the cup was returned to the saucer. Remove the cup and saucer together, and refill it behind the priest's right shoulder. Return the refilled cup in its saucer carefully to the table. What good luck--I had Speltz looking out for me again. To this day I can line up chairs perfectly, grasping either side of each chair and extending my thumbs to measure the length to the border of the table.

Herman's Work Shop... During the priest-waiter obedience, I asked Cy what he was painting in Herman's work shop, located in the junior's basement (old building), near the refectory. Earlier that October, in Herman's work shop, Cy

Andrew Stevans

had shown me how to make a Paper Mache mask for the large scarecrow with blinking eyes that welcomed all to the refectory for Halloween dinner.

He offered to show me the statues he had begun painting several weeks earlier for the Christmas scene at Sacred Heart Church. Following one of the lunch meals, we went down to the work shop. What an assemblage greeted us. There must have been two dozen, approximately 24" high statues, including sheep, cattle, shepherds, camels, wise men and a large angel. I offered to help Cy with the painting. He said he'd think about it.

Later, he let me paint the manger. What can you do to a manger?

ST. MARY'S COLLEGE, SAND PITS and SCIENCE FICTION

St. Mary's College had its own obvious attraction, not only for Notre Dame whose entire student body at the time was comprised of young college men, but for the Holy Cross senior chosen to select another senior to serve Sunday Mass at St. Mary's each week. This coveted obedience was Joe Schott's until his "demise," then became Jim Glaza's responsibility.

Each week, the "chosen one" selected another senior and these two went to St. Mary's to serve the Sunday Mass as Alter Boys. I was Glaza's selection.

That year, both Jim Glaza and I had become addicted to reading sci-fi short stories. Not those fantasy-type stories where fear, monsters, and flight are major elements, but the plausible science where there existed a remote possibility of the event happening somewhere in the cosmos. Even in the 1950's there seemed to be an endless supply of great sci-fi out there.

Let me explain sci-fi addiction. In each of the senior's shared rooms, there was a large, lighted, walk-in closet. After evening chapel and final studies, it was lights out. Andy Roering would go to bed. I, on the other hand, would go into the large walk-in closet, turn on the light, close the door, and sit and read sci-fi short stories until the wee hours. I understood from Glaza's roommate, John Butler, that Glaza did the same.

This went on for most of my senior year. When a new steam man was appointed, I was moved to Jim Callahan's room down the hall. At lights out Callahan would turn in. I would drag a chair into the closet, turn on the light, shut the door and continue my sci-fi readings.

One Sunday, while returning from St. Mary's, Glaza and I discovered something just to the right of St. Mary's Road. There were several sand pits among the grass and trees. The pits were on the St. Mary's campus and directly across the Dixie highway from the Holy Cross senior field. Following our serving Mass at St. Mary's, we would take a few quiet hours to lie in the sun and read the latest Ray Bradbury, or Theodore Sturgeon, or Clifford Simak. We may have missed First Sunday Devotions at Sacred Heart Church more than once. We felt little remorse.

The only thing that stopped our mutual addiction was graduation from Holy Cross. Late in our senior year, Glaza mentioned that he was determined to find out if flying saucers actually existed. To pursue his interest, he discussed possibly attending the new Air Force Academy in Colorado Springs, Colorado.

He did. They don't.

"SPRING CLEANING" ST. MARY'S LAKE

It was mid-May. The weather in Northern Indiana had been warm and humid the past week. Several of us seniors decided it was time to clean up St. Mary's Lake, around the St. Mary's pier.

The idea was to have three, two-man teams of Senior Life Guards. A team was assigned to either side of the pier, and one at the front, diving area of the pier. We planned to retrieve sticks, cans or jars thrown in St Mary's Lake during the fall and winter months by passers-by. We knew that in several weeks, our fellow classmates would be diving off the pier and swimming around the pier area. There was always the chance of someone stepping on a sharp stick or open can--or worse, the shards from a broken bottle.

We knew the water was cold, so we took the precaution of carrying our bathrobes to wear later, over our wet swim trunks. Twenty feet back from the pier was a structure with two dozen clothes hooks for hanging towels during normal swim season. We hung up our bathrobes and towels and entered the water.

We hadn't been in the water for more than a few minutes—it seemed much longer-- before we realized the water temperature was too low for swimming or maneuvering in the water. It felt well below the mid-50's of Lake Michigan, experienced during our annual June trip to Tower Hill. We decided to wait a week or two longer before attempting the cleaning operation again.

Upon leaving the water our bodies shook so badly we couldn't easily direct ourselves to our bathrobes. Several classmates, some of them on the house baseball team, had been watching the brief lake cleaning effort, and observed our weaving and drunk-like behavior, They had little empathy for our predicament, and laughed loudly.

At the time, it hadn't dawned on us that, a week earlier, while playing baseball against Moreau, there were snow flurries off-and-on during the game.

WASHING, WAXING, SQUEEGEE-ING

"Rheen-O-Sheening" Floors... The Holy Cross refectory, the dining hall for the entire house, was about 40 feet wide by 100 feet long. In addition to waiting tables, the refectory crew had a second obedience (work assignment), cleaning and waxing the refectory floor on a given Saturday. During the waiters' dinner the evening before, we established a cleaning crew and their assignments. One crew that comes to mind was comprised of Tom Norris, Dick Howard, Jerry Wood, Jude McCusker, Don Kaiser, Don Parks, Jim Callahan, Ed Whelan, Dave Gibson and Dick Cavanaugh.

Following breakfast or lunch, the team of 8 to 10 of us stacked tables and chairs at one end of the refectory. We then spread a mixture of liquid Fels Naptha soap and water with mops. We removed the old wax using a large, 24 inch, spinning electric brush, operated by hand. The brush acted almost like a sander, breaking through the old wax, down to the tiled floor.

After the thorough washing, a fresh coat of "Rheen O Sheen" wax was applied to the dry floor, spread uniformly with the mops, and then allowed to dry. Using the same buffer, but outfitted with a terry cloth cover--or an old towel--covering the brush, the buffer was used to shine the refectory floor to a high luster. Running the buffer took some practice, but soon many of us could control the large, cumbersome machine with one hand, easily reversing its direction.

After cleaning and waxing one half of the refectory, all tables and chairs were moved and stacked at the cleaned end of the refectory, and the same cleaning and waxing effort was made to complete the final half of the refectory. The job took several hours, but the results made the effort well worth it. You could literally eat off the floor. If allowed, and with the proper dare, a few of us worker-bees probably would have tried it.

We created the verb form of Rheen O Sheen. We would say we "Rheen O Sheened" the refectory, or, I just "Rheen O Sheened" the main corridor." This was most likely a term coined years earlier, and handed down by upper classmen to the next generation of Holy Cross waiters.

I recall that one late afternoon, on my first day at Bainbridge, MD, USNTC (boot camp), in September, 1955, a Chief Petty Officer asked if anyone knew how to run a buffer. In our group of 58 Pittsburgh recruits, no one raised their hand. I naively raised mine.

"Stevans, would you run the buffer and shine the hall floors up a bit?"

"Of course, sir," I said, and started the buffer. The group watched in silence—I was hoping it was in awe—as I used my one hand then a few fingers to control the back and forth motion of the buffer. It was a long 15 foot wide corridor. I may be wrong in my estimate, but the hall appeared to extend over 100 feet down one side of the building, then another 65 feet across the back, and 100 feet up to the front on the other side of the building. After what seemed like two hours, I had finally finished up and reported back to the Chief.

"Well, Stevans, you can re-join your Pittsburgh company, and report to the chow hall for dinner."

"By the way sir, how did you know my name?" I asked.

"I know everyone here, Stevans." He smiled. It was later that I realized my name was stenciled above the front left pocket and also across the back of my dungaree shirt.

Squeegee-ing Windows... Windows lined both sides and the far end of the Holy Cross refectory. The window cleaning chore typically fell to the waiters. Squeegee-ing windows required a lot of effort but held little appeal for most of us. You had to step up on a five-foot ladder to reach the top panes.

I recall two juniors, John Murphy, from Hornell, New York, and Conrad Henke a lanky kid from Tiffin, Ohio, both a year behind us, offering to do windows in the morning, before we Rheen O Sheened the refectory early that afternoon.

Murphy, a lumbering kid with big feet, appeared somewhat uncoordinated. He required Henke to hold onto the ladder. When Murphy still appeared unsteady on the ladder, Dan Panchot, an Oklahoman, volunteered to hold the other side of the ladder. But Murphy would literally walk off the ladder. Finally, Henke and Panchot teamed up to finish the job with Gerry Sheehan, another junior, hailing from Detroit, Michigan. Murphy was banished from the refectory before he became the first Holy Cross, five-foot ladder casualty.

It wasn't much later when Murphy fell off the recreation room pool table, hitting hard on the floor and breaking his arm. No one recalls why he was on the pool table. According to Jim Keating, the incident was reported in the *South Bend Tribune*.

Andrew Stevans

FIELD DAY

The 440 Relay... One of the final acts in our senior year at Holy Cross was an unforgettable Field Day event, held out at the senior field. There was a 440 relay race, a long jump (one junior jumped 26 feet—close to a world record), a shot put contest, and a baseball throw, among the many activities.

I trained for the 440 yard relay race by running the senior field base paths, daily. At the time, it didn't dawn on me that the base path yardage may be shorter than the yards I'd be required to run in the relay. Also, when running alone, without the pressure of classmates cheering me on, I was relaxed and loose during my practice runs.

The day of the event was warm and sunny, the senior field dry. The entire Holy Cross student body was there, along with a dozen resident priests. The 440 was measured off in the same part of the field as the baseball infield I had run each day, but it appeared longer. I arrived just as the 440 event began. I was designated the anchor for our team.

The event seemed to unfold so rapidly that I may not have been mentally prepared when the baton was off handed to me. We were ahead of Hines team by several yards. Ed was his team's anchor. I quickly sped around two-thirds of the course leaving the competition still rounding the first turn. Halfway down the final third, I could actually see the rope across the finish line, when my leg muscles froze. As hard as I tried, my legs wouldn't respond to my mental commands. The muscles felt knotted--a cramping effect.

In my peripheral vision I could see Hines approaching. He slowly caught up and passed me by. I don't recall anyone else passing me as I stumbled across the finish line, but I felt I had definitely let my team down. Years later, the comedian, Bill Cosby, would perfectly explain my dilemma when he described what happened to him toward the end of a race he ran at Temple University. It was a humbling experience for him as well. I felt fortunate that no one talked about my loss afterwards.

The Baseball throw had a collection of outfielders all vying for the honor of the longest throw. I knew right away who the major competitor would be. Len Biallas, a junior classmate from Pontiac Michigan, had a strong arm and thick wrists. Biallas could throw a side ball (not overhand), from third base to first with a simple snap of his wrist. That afternoon, he had a disconcerting confidence about him..
    We were gathered in the outfield, near St. Mary's Road throwing baseballs across the outfield toward St. Mary's Lake. We had two chances to make our longest throw. One of the priests at the far end of the outfield marked each throw.
    I threw last, just after Biallas. I knew how far he had thrown. He was ahead of the competition by several yards. I followed Father Brinker's advice from the previous year, taking a slight hop, landing on my left foot as leverage, and over handing the ball--hard. My first toss was close to Biallas longest throw, but not a winner. The second toss went past Biallas's, landing in the briars and weeds beyond the path to the outdoor basketball court.
    My legs let me down, earlier, I thought, but my throwing arm has made up for it. Yet, each time I recalled losing the 440 relay, I felt the pangs of remorse.

Andrew Stevans

POST HOLY CROSS YEARS

Father Harold Riley
Superior, Holy Cross Seminary

HOLY CROSS GRADUATION, THE SUMMER OF 1955

Following graduation from Holy Cross, most of the class spent the summer with family and friends, preparing for their Novitiate year in Jordan, Minnesota, a year of contemplation, prayer and farm labor, and the acceptance of their temporary vows of poverty, chastity and obedience.

There would be liturgical studies and discussion but no college subjects taught during that year, a rest from the study regimen at Holy Cross.

I was from Pittsburgh, Pennsylvania, and would be the only class member from Holy Cross to spend my Novitiate year at Bennington, Vermont, the Eastern Province novitiate. I had played catch-up in studies for three years at Holy Cross and was tired of a study regimen. A novitiate year, free of studies, was a God send.

During my senior-year final Visiting Sunday, Father Riley called my parents and me into his office. He explained that I would attend two years at Stonehill College in North Easton, Massachusetts before taking my Novitiate year.

Father Riley was respected as friend and confidant by all who knew him. In my eyes he was more a Holy Cross chaplain than a superior. I thought he'd accept my rationale.

I listened until Father completed his dictum, took a deep breath and explained my desire to attend novitiate year first, then justified my request by elaborating on my mental fatigue from studies and my playing catch up since joining Holy Cross in the sophomore year. I urged Father to consider sending me to my novitiate year, first.

Father listened patiently then lectured me on the soon-to-be-taken vow of obedience. I then mentioned the obvious, that all other Holy Cross seniors, my classmates, were Western Province and would attend Novitiate year that fall in Jordan Minnesota, before returning to their study regimen at Notre Dame. But, nothing more was discussed. Father talked cordially with the parents for a few minutes and we were dismissed. I wondered how many other meetings he would have with my classmates and their parents. Maybe some would not make it to Jordan, but would be dismissed following Holy Cross graduation.

After arriving home in Pittsburgh, I mailed a carefully prepared letter to Father Riley, again requesting that I be allowed to attend Novitiate year first, like the rest of my classmates, re-explaining my rationale. In a most pleasant response, Father Riley denied my request. I then formally declined the invitation to attend Stonehill College.

While finishing my last weeks at Holy Cross, I had been invited by Jim Glaza to visit his home in Bay City, Michigan, and by Lee Skinner to visit his home in Chicago, Illinois.The following week, I departed Pittsburgh for Bay City, Michigan.

Bay City, Michigan... What a time we had. Jim Glaza, with his outgoing personality, was a natural for scheduling a series of activities. Daily, a carload of friends accompanied us to the beach on Lake Huron, or to the Saginaw City Fair, or a band session in his garage that spilled out onto his driveway. Did I mention that during this time, his folks were on vacation in the Eastern Upper Peninsula of Michigan, touring islands such as Mackinac, a Victorian hideaway almost without communication to the outside world? This was a most perfect situation for us.

An aside... The 1979 movie "Somewhere in Time," starring Christopher Reeve and Jane Seymour, was filmed at the Grand Hotel on Mackinac Island. Mackinac Island greeted visitors with

"*where every day is timeless,
every night precious*"

The greeting originated following the popularity of the movie.

Steve, a gangly, tough teen neighbor had a "Rebel Without a Cause" personality and was one of the bunch. Steve, Jim and I, along with a few girls from the neighborhood, possibly Donna Carlin and Patty, Jim's sister, and her friend, attended the Saginaw Fair one evening. We lost quite a few dollars trying to win a portable radio. Steve caught the carnival guy performing a slight-of-hand and grabbed him. In a flash the man yelled "RUBE," and was gone, radio and all. We decided to leave the fair early.

During that very busy week, we didn't take much time out to eat, and got very few hours of rest. In the later part of the week, Pat offered to wash Jim's and my clothes. She returned the clean, neatly folded clothes and teased me about my ragged T-shirts. I laughed and commented that they had to last another few years, and I hoped she hadn't used too much bleach.

Jim's folks arrived home the following day. They were quiet people. His dad was pleasant enough. His mom was less than pleased with the condition of the house—we had occupied every square foot except for Patty's bedroom, where she and her girlfriend hung out. Jim explained persuasively that the older brother, Tom's room in the attic, outfitted with a drafting table and bed were not in disarray to any extent at all. Neither Jim nor I could understand his mother's exasperation. The following day, I departed for Dearborn to have lunch with my aunt, then continued on to Chicago, leaving Jim to justify, rationalize—and attend to his "obedience," cleaning up the house.

Chicago, Illinois... Lee Skinner and his parents met me at the Chicago train station. They were pleased to see me, and, on the way home treated me to pizza. I think the Pizza place may have been the first Uno's Chicago Grill, well before Uno's spread across the country. It was the first time I had tasted a Pizza. To this day, I can attest that it was one of the best tasting pizzas I've had.

The following day Lee invited me to visit the Chicago beach on Lake Michigan, a good 100 miles across the southern end of the lake from The Dunes and Tower Hill, where he, I and our Holy Cross classmates had spent so many memorable days.

Swimming was a part of us after spending several years living near St. Mary's Lake. We both had secured "the Patch" in Senior Life Saving. Since I was scheduled to leave for Pittsburgh the following morning, we decided to wring every moment of enjoyment out of the short visit and headed for the beach immediately after breakfast.

As we arrived, Lee warned me that the Chicago side of Lake Michigan was unlike the sloping sand beaches and dunes on the eastern side of the lake at Tower Hill. We parked and walked across a wide grassy and treed area, then approached a line of large, smooth, dark colored boulders stretching along the shore as far as the eye could see. Lee explained that the boulders acted as a sea wall to protect erosion from the heavy rain storms and ice tides of winter. He assured me that the sand below the boulders was every bit as white and inviting as the sands of Tower Hill. I tested the waters a number of times, diving to the sandy bottom and following the boulders along the shore.

During that day at the beach, I mentioned to Lee the antics my brother Norm, a senior, and I encountered from juniors during my first trip to Tower Hill three years earlier. Lee was entertained with the account and we both reminisced about Holy Cross.

Lee later pointed to a work-out area (a muscle beach) in the park near the beach, and related some of the spontaneous wrestling and boxing that went on there. I was surprised to see both men and women worked out with weights.

Andrew Stevans

After a leisurely afternoon, we joined Lee's family for some home cooking, and retired late. The following morning, Lee and his family accompanied me to the train station. We sat in the car for a short period, discussing Lee and my upcoming novitiate year. Lee was the first to know my plan to join the Navy later in the summer.

While I was in the Navy, Lee Skinner and I stayed in touch during his novitiate and early years at Notre Dame. In the spring of 1960, Jim Glaza invited me to his Air Force Academy graduation. He was in the second graduating class of the new academy.

PREP SCHOOL DAYS The Seminary at the University of Notre Dame

---

Paisano: Ski trip, the Abetone Forest, Italy

SKIING IN ITALY...
A CHANCE ENCOUNTER

Abetone Forest... During a cruise with the 6th Fleet in the Mediterranean ("the Med"), all expenses paid by the U.S. Government, my ship, the U.S.S. Heermann--a 376 foot, 2200 ton destroyer--moored to the landing in Leghorn (a.k.a. Livorno), Italy. Leghorn is located a short distance from Pisa with its famed Leaning Tower, and seven hours from Rome.

At mail call, I received a letter from Lee Skinner in which he mentioned that Father Paul Rankin, a former English teacher, was appointed the new superior at Moreau Seminary and had invited me to visit at a future date. Skinner wrote that Gene Gorski, the Baritone, and Tom McNally, a UPI correspondent were in his class. I began day dreaming about my Holy Cross experiences, and my many friends at Moreau, promising that one day I'd return to Notre Dame for a visit.

It was a cool Sunday in January. As in most ports in the Med, tours were offered to the ships company. A friend and I accepted a one-day opportunity to visit the Abetone Forest region, extended to all hands by the U.S. Army. Abetone was a well known ski resort area, located a few hours by bus from Livorno.

At 0630 the following morning a U.S. Army bus stopped by the ship. The bus was already half-filled with Army men and women. Three of us boarded for the trip, outfitted in our Navy issue turtleneck sweaters, double socks pulled up over the legs of double dungarees and tied with string to keep the snow out of our boondockers--Navy issue boots. This outfit was "topped off" with the U.S. Navy sock hat.

We arrived at the Abetone snow line at 8:30 a.m., and stopped above a mountain stream to put on chains. A tiny car—we called them cracker boxes—slid while descending the hill and rammed the front of the bus. It did no damage to the bus, but the trunk door of the car was on the ground and its fender smashed. A few of us helped move the damaged car to the side of the road. The bus driver offered the occupants a drive back up to the ski lodge which they accepted.

We continued up the mountain. The road angled, and as the bus swung out to make the turn we met a large truck coming down from the ski resort. The truck slid toward the bus. The two vehicles wedged themselves tightly together. Our group moved to the back of the bus, allowing the truck to loosen itself by backing up. We continued to the top of the mountain and the ski resort, arriving at 11:00.

I was hungry. My shipmate friends from the Heermann and I ordered a spaghetti meal. The spaghetti and ground beef were served mixed together, the sauce and cheese on top. We were served table wine and thin sliced Italian bread. The meal was delicious and cost just 35 cents. In the States at the time the meal would have cost $2.00.

After eating, my friends and I rented skis, boots and poles for $1.50. It took 12 minutes by ski-lift to reach the top of the hill, and 30 minutes for us to fall back down the hill. Fearing we'd kill ourselves, we then trudged up a less aggressive hill that had no lift, but had a path with concrete steps.

With snow blowing in my face, I began to ski the smaller hill and literally ran down a man who was carrying his skis. He had hurt his ankle and was attempting to cross the snow to the walking path. He introduced himself as Tom Gorman with the U.S. Army, originally from South Bend, Indiana. What a surprise. Gorman worked at the Old College building when it was being used as a mission house and a rendezvous point for Holy Cross American missionaries. I mentioned my association with Notre Dame. He became excited at the mention of Father O'Donnell, and explained that, at one time, he had lived near Father O'Donnell on Notre Dame Avenue. He also knew Father Riley and some of the priests at the Little Sem.

I helped Gorman down the hill to the restaurant where the resort had a first aid station. Gorman's ankle was iced for a half hour then wrapped with an ACE bandage. During the first aid, Gorman and I entertained my shipmates with stories of Notre Dame football and Holy Cross.

Gorman planned to remain at Abetone for another day before heading down the mountain. My Navy friends and I joined him for our second spaghetti meal and some additional camaraderie. I remained with Gorman until the bus was loading for the return trip. We shook hands and I wished him luck with the ankle.

My shipmates and I departed Abetone at 1700 (5:00 p.m.), arriving in Pisa at 8:20 p.m., and reporting back on board the Heermann at 2100 (9:00 p.m.).

> An aside... On an earlier Med (Mediterranean) cruise the U.S.S. Heermann was designated the U.S. representative to the Grace Kelly/Prince Rainier wedding. In the first year (1956) that I was on board, the U.S.S. Heermann was invited back during Christmas, when Monaco was anticipating the birth of Princess Caroline. It snowed on Christmas Eve, the only snow fall we experienced that year in the Mediterranean.
> On January 23, 1957, when little Caroline was born, the Heermann had already departed Monaco anchorage and joined in maneuvers with the French Navy off the coast of Italy.

ROME, ITALY

Mike Novak, CSC

Andy Stevans, USN

VISITING ROME

Collegio di Santa Croce... The week following our Abetone adventure, the ships company was offered a 3-day trip to Rome. I wanted to visit oldest brother, Jack's, classmate, Mike Novak, CSC, originally from the Pittsburgh area and Holy Cross. Novak was at the Collegio di Santa Croce, so I signed up for the Rome tour along with shipmates from several of the ships in our squadron.

During the eight-hour bus trip, nearly an inch of snow fell, but stopped as we reached the outskirts of Tuscany. The food in Tuscany was delicious, even though it was only steak and eggs, toast and coffee. This meal was popular in Italy and apparently was the meal of choice for the tour. We continued on. The snow disappeared completely off the roads as the bus continued south to Rome.

Andrew Stevans

Arriving in Rome in the early afternoon, we registered at the Hotel Columbia. In the hotel restaurant Mario Lanza could be heard singing on the radio.

I called Novak from the lobby phone. At his suggestion I boarded the number 64 cross city bus from Viminale to St. Peter's Square and walked the short distance to Holy Cross College. There, I was introduced to several of older brother, Jack's, classmates, Jim Burtchaell, Nick Ayo, and Tom Walsh ("Little Tom"), and Father Martin from the Eastern Province Novitiate at Bennington, Vermont, and to one of my brother, Norm's, friends, Gerry Quirk.

All were cut ups. We had an enjoyable time reminiscing about Holy Cross, the various resident priests-- two former Holy Cross superiors, Fathers Richard Grimm and John Collins, whom I barely knew, and their personality quirks. The group easily matched me with their anecdotes on Holy Cross life, describing in detail the many pranks they pulled while at the Little Sem.

Novak and I departed for St. Mary Major (Santa Maria Maggiore) to view the fascinating mosaics in the ceiling and behind the alter. I think Father Simmons would have enjoyed being there.

We made several additional stops on a walking tour of the area Churches to view other mosaics. During the late afternoon we stopped for a light meal and discussed our parents back in Pennsylvania who knew each other through the Holy Cross Lay Family meetings. We discussed where our lives had taken us and the coincidences that brought Mike and me to Rome at the same time.

Novak had to return to the college to attend 6:30 chapel, so we parted company, hailed separate taxis and I returned to the hotel.

That evening, several of my Navy shipmates and I decided to attend the movie "Il Cavalieri Senza Volto" translated "The Lone Ranger." The sound track was in Italian and the theatre was full of smokers, but we stayed through the entire movie.

Tonto didn't say "Kimo Sabe" (trusted friend). He addressed the Lone Ranger as "paisano." There were other laughable phrases in the movie that escape my memory.

The following day, we toured the old Roman Coliseum, the Catacombs, the Olympic Stadium that held 70,000 people, the famous "Three Coins" fountain, the Vatican Museum and library, the Sistine Chapel, and Italy's largest memorial, dedicated to Victor Emmanuel. In San Pietro (St. Peter's) Square we viewed a life-like statue of The Infant of Prague.

Overall, the Italian experience became a highlight of my Mediterranean tour.

Following our meeting in Rome, Mike began a serious writing career as novelist and journalist. Novak is originally from Johnstown, Pennsylvania, where both his parents and mine belonged to the Pittsburgh Holy Cross Lay-Family group. In 1960, the Novak's attended Louise and my wedding in Pittsburgh, Pennsylvania.

GEIST RESERVOIR, FORTVILLE, INDIANA

Joe Schott & wife, Andy Stevans and wife: 1966

VISITING CENTRAL INDIANA and NOTRE DAME: 1966

The Trip to Indiana... During August of 1966, my wife, Louise, and I decided to take a 10-day trip, leaving from the Finger Lakes region of New York and driving to Indianapolis's Geist Reservoir (Fortville, Indiana area) to visit with Louise's sister and brother-in-law for several days. We took our four year old son, Dale, and baby, Michelle with us. I planned a get together with Joe Schott.

Following the visit to Fortville, we would proceed north on State 31 to Notre Dame to spend a few days at Holy

PREP SCHOOL DAYS The Seminary at the University of Notre Dame

Cross visiting with Father Fiedler, then return to our home in New York.

I recall very little about the trip from Indianapolis to Notre Dame, or our return trip from South Bend to the Finger Lakes. But the trip from New York to the Indianapolis area remains fresh in memory. Getting to Indianapolis was an adventure in itself.

Early on, we had prepared for the trip by having an air conditioner installed in our 1963 Chevy Bel Air. Back then, air conditioning was not a standard feature in many cars. The air conditioning unit was the best I've owned, attested to by a number of air conditioning mechanics, who, at first questioned the low readings coming from the unit. On the trip we were unaware of the reliability of the new air conditioner. We quickly covered the 200 miles of I-90 West, from Canandaigua across the Southern Tier of New York, along Pennsylvania's scenic Lake Erie, and to the I-271 Cleveland South bypass.

We paid dearly for our leisurely drive along Lake Erie, managing to hit Cleveland in the middle of rush hour on one of the hottest days of the year. According to the local news, the humidity was near 80 percent. Those driving near us, many with car windows rolled down, looked red-faced, sweaty and frustrated at the bumper-to-bumper mess. Little son, Dale, was asleep in a make-shift bed in the back seat. Baby Michelle was in a car bed. Louise had opened an umbrella to protect the children from the direct heat of the glaring sun through the back car window.

We were hoping to reach Fortville, Indiana, and the Geist Reservoir area that day. Yet, we crept along on the Cleveland beltway for over an hour-and-a-half, passing overheated cars that had pulled off, or were kindly pushed off, to the side of the road. The situation became tense when we discovered few exits along the beltway. Rest stops seemed non-existent along that section of road.

In the south of Cleveland we managed to outpace the heaviest traffic and soon had a straight shot down I-71 to Columbus, Ohio. We ate dinner, called the in-laws, and stayed at a Columbus hotel for the night.

The following morning was overcast and raining. Fog covered the western side of the partially constructed I-270 Columbus beltway, as well as the first 20 miles or so of old Route 40/I-70 West. Slowly the morning rain and fog disbursed. The remainder of the trip was overcast but uneventful.

Geist Reservoir... Upon reaching Fortville, we followed directions to the Geist Reservoir, a 10 mile long, one mile wide lake, a few miles west of the Indianapolis Airport. The lake had forest land on both sides. I understood that hunting, often illegal, was a problem around the reservoir area, as was fishermen using dynamite to illegally catch fish.

It was not unusual to have game wardens shot in the area. Louise's brother in law, Bill Smith, was well known and respected both in the local neighborhood and in Fortville. Twice, Bill had held the title of Regional Small Bore Rifle Champion. He patrolled the lake in a fiber glass boat with twin outboard 90 HP engines.

That day he and I shot many rounds at several distant targets. Bill showed me how to use a spotting scope. We shot 22 long-rifle rounds using the gun Bill used to win the Regional championships.

PREP SCHOOL DAYS The Seminary at the University of Notre Dame

Louise's sister, Lee, had planned a cook out the following day and Bill asked if I would invite the Schotts to join us at the cook out, and enjoy some swimming and water skiing, and, of course, to reminisce about old times at Holy Cross.

The following afternoon, Schott and I met. It had been over 10 years. He appeared in great physical condition, mentioning that he was a High School coach, and, earlier had a three-year stint in the Air Force. I introduced Joe and his wife to Lee, Bill and Louise. We then settled in for a most enjoyable and memorable day.

Following lunch, we had a relaxed conversation about Holy Cross classmates and Jim Glaza, at the time a Captain in the Air Force and a graduate of the new Air Force Academy in Colorado Springs, Colorado. I mentioned to Schott that, after he had departed Holy Cross, Glaza assumed his obedience (assignment) as St. Mary's College Mass server and I was asked to accompany him weekly to St. Mary's. Schott and Bill had a hearty laugh hearing about Glaza's and my addiction to science fiction reading and our hanging out at the St. Mary's College sand pits after mid morning Mass, to indulge the "addiction."

Bill endured the many Holy Cross stories and finally invited us and the wives to accompany him on his boat and spend the rest of the afternoon water skiing and patrolling the reservoir. Neither Schott nor I had water skied before, but, with Bill's careful guidance, we both quickly became adept at skiing in the boat's wake, then skiing across the wake, and from side to side. Schott was on the skis as we approached the Geist Reservoir overpass. Bill slowed and proceeded under the overpass. It took us a moment to realize that Schott had sunk with his skis, and was left floating in his life jacket far behind.

Visiting with Schott was like visiting with a brother. That evening we spent another few hours reminiscing on Bill's enclosed back porch. We described our seminary lives at Notre Dame, providing many examples of our "Little Sem" antics.

Bill described Louise and my 1960 wedding, and his visit to Pittsburgh with Lee, his wife, and Kitty, both older sisters of Louise. I explained to Schott that Bill accompanied Louise up the isle, standing in for her recently departed father. We shared photographs and memories through the late evening hours. Although years had passed, Schott and I agreed, it felt as though we had seen each other just yesterday.

HOLY CROSS, NOTRE DAME, INDIANA, 1966

Dale, Frs. Knoll & Fiedler   **Dale, manning the entrance gate**

Holy Cross at Notre Dame... **E**arly the following morning, we bid adieu to Lee and Bill and departed Fortville, Indiana to drive north to South Bend on Route 31. After checking into a hotel, I called Holy Cross and asked Father

Simmons if I could stop by with the family to visit with Father Fiedler and Father Sowala. Fr. Simmons was surprised to hear from me, but urged me to stop by that afternoon. I mentioned to Father that we would tour the Notre Dame campus first, then, with any luck, reach Fr. Sowala and have a chat with Rog. Fr. Simmons said he would pass my request on to Fr. Fiedler, and let him track down Roger.

After lunch, we drove casually around the Notre Dame campus. I noticed an unusual site, a new building near the stadium (Hesburgh Library) with what appeared to be a three or four story mural beautifully designed on the outside of the building. We stopped at the book store and the campus cafeteria where, years earlier the parents and I had enjoyed long lunch conversations during their Holy Cross Visits. I drove the family to Sacred Heart Church and the Grotto **(photo #1)**, and snapped a photo of Holy Cross Seminary, looking northeast across St. Mary's Lake, and showing the newly planted trees on the sloping front lawn **(photo #2)**.

Aside from the newly planted trees, everything appeared pretty much as I had remembered. As we approached the north side of the Holy Cross, Fr. Fiedler was there, grinning and waving to us. Several seminarians were laughing with Father but dismissed themselves as we parked.

I introduced the family. The first thing I noticed differently about Father Fiedler was his ability to hear everything I was saying. He explained his new hearing aid was far better than the old one. He considered his hearing near 100%. Father proceeded to give us a short walking tour of the grounds, introducing us to several of the resident priests. They all appeared to be around my age.

Father and I discussed my life's journey to date—the Navy, my trip to Rome to visit Novak, my education and marriage, even the recent purchase of the Old School House in North Greece, New York, a historic site, that he seemed particularly interested in. We discussed briefly the baptism of my children and a young CSC priest in North Greece, temporarily assigned to the local Catholic parish.

But I really wanted to talk about my classmates and what Father knew of their lives. It turned out Father had bits and pieces of information but was obviously fully absorbed with the current batch of young candidates for the priesthood. We both began reminiscing about sports and unforgettable wins. Father said he still continued to play some handball and pick-up football. As we talked outside the building, near the freshman/sophomore locker rooms more than one seminarian spoke to Father, and engaged him in conversation, a few times out of earshot. I truly felt like I'd returned home to the family of Holy Cross.

While Father went inside to attempt to reach Sowala again by phone, I walked across the junior field to the spot where, years earlier, Mulkerin had left me at the end our infamous race around St. Joe Lake. I took a photo of the playing field looking toward Holy Cross House and our parked Chevy Bel Air **(photo #3)**.

On Father Fiedler's return, he had a surprise. Fathers Pete Sandonato and Jerry Knoll had joined Father Fiedler to welcome us. Both priests took an interest in Dale, our oldest son, who was four at the time. I assured Father that Dale was interested in everything that his dad had done at Holy Cross, including (and in particular) fishing St. Mary's Lake.

Father Sandonato told Dale that, like his dad, he was from Pittsburgh, Pennsylvania, and that his parents (Frank and

PREP SCHOOL DAYS The Seminary at the University of Notre Dame

Rose Sandonato) had attended his dad and mom's wedding. That level of relationship confused Dale. He looked mystified and we all laughed. Dale would be attending Kindergarten the next spring so Father Sandonato and I told Dale a few anecdotes about the strict grade school nuns we had as teachers in elementary school.

Pictures were taken. There were departing comments and blessings from both priests. It was the last time I would enjoy their company.

The family and I drove around the property trying to locate some of the remaining tree stumps belonging to the felled trees Klouda and I had cut up into manageable pieces over 12 years earlier **(photo #4)**. All traces were gone.

We then continued up St. Mary's Road to the Priests' cemetery. I took a photo, looking southwest, across the senior playing field toward Our Lady of Fatima Shrine and the Dixie Highway **(photo #5)**. I then made an about-face (180 degree turn) and took the final photo, looking southeast, across the Priests' cemetery toward Holy Cross **(photo #6)**.

The senior field looked exactly as I had remembered. At the far end of the field, near the Shrine, was the baseball diamond and the site of the Field Day Long-Jump and 440 yard Relay Race. Closest to the camera was the site of the Baseball Throw.

Brother Seraphim's "melon patch" was located directly across St. Mary's Road from the Priest's cemetery and the Senior field. It does not appear in the photo.

I related a kid friendly version of the melon patch story to Dale. He understood all too well, and asked when we were going to eat.

Photos… During the 1966 visit to Holy Cross

(1) Grotto, looking east from Holy Cross Seminary entrance

(2) St. Mary's Lake, looking west: Holy Cross front Lawn

PREP SCHOOL DAYS The Seminary at the University of Notre Dame

(3) Junior Field looking southwest toward Holy Cross House (The "Unofficial end" of the race around St. Joe Lake)

(4) The Junior Field looking south, from St. Mary's Road

Andrew Stevans

(5) Priest's cemetery: looking southwest across the Senior Field

(6) Priests' cemetary: looking southeast toward Holy Cross

PREP SCHOOL DAYS The Seminary at the University of Notre Dame

Courtesy of Bill and Mary Lou Klouda

NOTE:
At the end of the 1966/1967 school-year, Holy Cross Seminary closed its doors. Holy Cross became a Notre Dame students' residence hall. In 1996 Holy Cross was demolished.

Andrew Stevans

THE 2000 REUNION

...Moreau Seminary...
HOLY CROSS CLASS OF 1955
(NOTRE DAME CLASS OF 1960)

(Courtesy of Jim Keating)
BACK ROW: Jim Keating, Dave Gibson, Br. Bill Tomes, Jerry Wood, Fr. John Croston (our host), and Tom Norris.

FRONT ROW: Tom Hayes, Andy Stevans, Jack Gilligan, Jim Callahan, and Bill Norris.

First Day... Initially, the invitation was extended by Tom Norris. A reunion was planned in the fall of 2000 for all Holy Cross classmates. The get-together would coincide with the now famous Nebraska/Notre Dame football game. We were invited to stay at Moreau Seminary, the home of the

Western Province seminarians while attending Notre Dame. Moreau is located across St. Joe Lake from the former Holy Cross grounds.

On an afternoon flight from Washington, DC to South Bend, there was some rowdy behavior on the part of several drunken alumni. I rationalized that they were Nebraska alumni. It wasn't a pretty sight and I'm sure their antics did not impress the other passengers, many continuing on to Chicago. One look at the disgust on some of their faces, including the stewardesses made me realize that, regardless of the school they (mis)represented, these thoughtless alumni had just given Notre Dame a black eye.

Upon landing, there was a rush to exit. For a moment I thought I spotted Cy Speltz disembarking with another gentleman, but was unable to catch up to them.

I watched for Cy at the luggage pick up. Then, hoping to see him at the car rental counters, I hung around for a bit before finally driving out to the Notre Dame campus.

Arriving at Moreau, I parked in a spot across the macadam from the rear entrance, and entered the house. After checking in for a room number at the prefect's office, I took a hot, small elevator to the second floor, left my bag in an uncomfortably warm room, returned to my car and drove out to the Dixie Highway to Walgreens in search of a fan.

Upon returning to Moreau, I met Washington DC friend and former Holy Cross roommate, Jim Callahan. He and I decided to take the short walk over to the Holy Cross Community Cemetery (priests' cemetery) to view some of our old friends and confidants; priests like Frs. Fiedler and Sandonato, who had served Holy Cross and its seminarians so well over the years.

PREP SCHOOL DAYS The Seminary at the University of Notre Dame

While touring the more recent graves, a rotund gentleman waved and approached quickly from the middle of the cemetery, smiling and exclaiming, "Hello, Hello. Who have we here?" Callahan and I immediately recognized the voice of Tom Hayes. What a delight to see his energetic presence and smiling face. Hayes, Callahan and I spoke quietly for some time about the newer grave stones with the names of priests who were our spiritual advisors and friends from so many years ago. Some I didn't recognize since I was not with Hayes and Callahan during their Novitiate and Notre Dame years.

With Mr. Hayes we returned to Moreau, and ran into a small group in the hallway preparing to go to dinner. Though it had been 45 years since we had seen each other, I immediately recognized Tom Norris and Jerry Wood by sight.

Jerry Wood and Tom Norris introduced us to their wives. We joined them, walking casually the short distance to the refectory. Dave Gibson and Jim Keating were already in the refectory with their wives. What a pleasant group we had. I experienced a feeling similar to the one I had when first meeting my classmates in the junior locker room so many years earlier.

Norris waved Father John Croston over, and introduced Father as our host for the next few days. We sat at a collection of round and square tables, pushed toward each other so we could chat about our lives since Holy Cross days.

I mentioned that while they were at the Western Novitiate in Jordan, Minnesota, and at Notre Dame, I was serving a six-year commitment in the Navy on a destroyer and then on a heavy cruiser, as part of the Atlantic Fleet.

The conversation changed. Callahan mentioned that some years earlier, Jerry Wood had stayed at Holy Cross House in Deep Creek, Maryland.

> An aside… On leave from the Navy in the late 1950's I had visited Deep Creek with brother, Norm, and our family. We cruised Deep Creek in a large "liberty launch" accompanied by my sister and two younger brothers. Later, we enjoyed the wonderful company of the men at Holy Cross House, joining a group gathered around a piano, singing light opera scores.

The discussion turned to the Eastern Province of Holy Cross, the novitiate in Bennington, Vermont and Stonehill College, the "Notre Dame of the East," located in North Easton, Massachusetts. Someone brought up the undefeated heavyweight boxing champ, Rocky Marciano, a devout Catholic. He was from nearby Brockton, Massachusetts. Part of his preparation for a fight was to visit the Grotto or Chapel at Stonehill College or attend St. Patrick's Church and pray to St. Anthony. Marciano would be seen doing his fitness runs around the campus.

> An aside… In the late summer of 1955, my father and I visited North Easton, and toured the Stonehill campus with my brother, Norm Stevans, CSC. Norm took us to the Ames Pond and to the railroad tracks behind the college. Everywhere you looked there was damage from a recent hurricane. Mature trees were thrown to the ground, their roots often extending well above our heads. Large, slate roof tiles were everywhere, half buried in the ground. Railroad cars were tossed like toys, and many homes and buildings were demolished or had roofs missing. A tidal wave couldn't have caused more damage.

PREP SCHOOL DAYS The Seminary at the University of Notre Dame

Norm Stevans, CSC, Stonehill College, Fall, 1956
Pius X Seminary

Following dinner at Moreau, the group retired to a large meeting room assigned to us near the refectory and continued our discussion about our individual journeys since 1955. Jim Keating had brought a kind of time machine: several volumes of black and white photos covering our years at Holy Cross. Until late in the evening, anecdotes were shared as we went photo by photo through the albums. The wives took photos of the men attendees, and the men took photos of the wives. We planned to mail a packet of all prints to attendees upon returning home. The group retired to their individual rooms, promising to meet in the refectory once again the following morning for breakfast.

Friday Night, before the big game... I joined up with Jim Callahan, Jerry and Maria Wood, and Tom Hayes to drive over to the Notre Dame book store, to find some souvenirs. We also accepted an offer from Tom Hayes to present us the "Hayes family tour" of Notre Dame. Tom was a second generation Notre Damer, and wanted to show us where his parents were married by his Uncle Tom, CSC. In the semi-darkness, at Hayes request, we drove into the cemetery near Notre Dame's main entrance gate. Hayes provided us a tour of the graveyard near the main gate pointing out an almost lost grave marker of Leon Hart, the Notre Dame All American, and his wife. What a time we had, with Tom's endless story telling and humorous anecdotes.

The Nebraska/Notre Dame Football Game... Bill Norris mentioned that, during the 1990's, Holy Cross House could no longer be maintained as suitable housing for students. The building had been condemned and was later demolished. I was anxious to see the grounds, and to view the Butler Building where we had taken our last two years of classes, held choir practices to prepare for our Christmas tour of South Bend, played many games of basketball and handball, and presented the light operas "Oklahoma" and "H.M.S. Pinafore."

I drove over to the Butler Building the following day. The edifice was still standing. Trees and shrubbery overgrew the large, one story facility and it was fairly well hidden in the woods. Over the years it had been converted to an art studio for the Notre Dame teaching staff, still useful in its old age.

Following morning Mass, the group met for breakfast in the Moreau refectory. Everyone was up for the Notre Dame-Nebraska game. We heard later that more Cornhuskers (red-clad fans) were in the stands for the game than Notre Damers (green-clad fans). No mention was made of the many hundreds of fans crowding the indoor large-screens outside the stadium entrances.

There's no other way to state this... Notre Dame lost to Nebraska 27 to 24 and Notre Dame ended the season with 9 wins - 3 losses to Nebraska's season of 10 wins – 2 losses. The game was attended by the largest crowd in Notre Dame's history.

Dave Gibson, his wife and I drove across campus to the stadium, and watched the game on one of the indoor screens. Following the game, Mrs. Gibson decided to avoid all the car traffic and walk back to Moreau. To avoid the bulk of traffic, Dave and I drove off campus, then back on campus through another gate. Mrs. Gibson, doing her few mile hike, easily beat us back to Moreau and was awaiting Dave when we arrived.

That Evening... As the others began arriving at Moreau we attended dinner. Jim Keating discovered a problem with Walgreen's incomplete development of his film, so following dinner, after everyone retired to their rooms to rest up for the evening get-together, Jim and I drove up the Dixie Highway to the local Walgreens to see if they would re-develop the negative film. After a few hours of negotiation and much patience, the effort paid off with excellent results on new sets of positive prints.

We arrived back at Moreau and Tom Hayes disappeared to his room. The rest of us joined the get-together in the air conditioned meeting room. Many topics were discussed during the waning evening hours. A major discussion centered on Brother Bill Tome's tireless efforts in the Chicago Cabrini district, where gangs, many of them Catholics known to the Brother, needed a mediator to arrange truces and meetings among gang leaders. Brother Tomes mentioned that, over time, the inter-gang hatreds disappeared. Many members left the gangs and returned to school or found jobs. Peace returned to the Cabrinni District.

It was almost midnight when a bedraggled soul in a night gown staggered through the Moreau meeting room door. It was Tom Hayes complaining of the heat and his inability to sleep. He threatened to retire to the choir loft of the chapel where there was air conditioning. Tom finally gave up his quest for rest, dressed, said goodbye to the group, and drove back to Saginaw, Michigan. Several of us walked Hayes to his air conditioned Buick and wished him off. It was a perfect ending to an entertaining evening with old friends who had once again become like extended family.

The following morning, following Mass and breakfast, I shook hands with my old classmates and departed Notre Dame, returning home to the family in Northern Virginia.

END

ACKNOWLEDGEMENTS

Father William (Bill) Simmons, CSC, volunteered in August, 2011 to begin the editing process, *"While I do not know precisely what kind of editing is needed, I was certainly on hand at Holy Cross Seminary in those days* (Father was Holy Cross superior for six years)*, and am willing to offer some suggestions and comments."*

Blessed with an alert and capable mind, Father launched into the editing effort and within a week had offered suggestions to make the memoires more readable by a non-Holy Cross audience. He found several redundancies, and recommended the elimination of a few unrelated paragraphs in the first essay. I imagine I was graded on the effort and most likely received a B- or a C, if I was lucky.

Father Leonard Banas, CSC, spiritual advisor during my senior year at Holy Cross, made many recommendations, both spiritually and temporally, during the Holy Cross writing project. Early on, Father recommended several Notre Dame faculty members for editing support--individuals who also had attended Holy Cross Seminary.

Father Banas's attention to my writing effort most likely brought to mind the incident mentioned in "The Soiree."

Father Tom Blantz, CSC, attempted to fit the editing job into his busy schedule. Finally, he emailed back explaining that with classes resuming and two other promised editing assignments still to complete, he was unable to do other than read some of the collection.

Father did, in fact, read the first 20 essays. He became excited that we both shared similar "obediences" at Holy Cross including our assignments as *steam men. *"Do keep up your work"* was Father's parting email comment.

NOTE: Steam men fed a large coal furnace, located in a separate building, that produced steam heat to registers located throughout Holy Cross.

Jim Callahan, a kind and concerned Holy Cross classmate and my senior year room mate, offered encouragement during the 1990's to "put pen to paper". This carried over to our 45th, 2000 Notre Dame reunion. Of course, Jim knew my curious nature. He may even have used my own rational to finally persuade me to begin the writing project.

Following receipt of the first 35 essays, Jim sent an email in July 2011: *"It makes me nostalgic for all that we had in those days at Holy Cross; days of close friendships and camaraderie.* Jim's running commentary during the heavy writing period of February through August contributed greatly to my inspiration and to the firm determination to complete the project.

Tom Hayes, a former classmate and our Holy Cross senior class president, took an immediate interest in the memoire writing project. As Tom completed reading a group of essays he'd handwrite his often copious and entertaining comments, (these sent by U.S. mail), along with old Province news articles and even a sheet of four-part music.

Tom's memory for the detail "back then," was indispensable in presenting events accurately. One remark of many that comes to mind, *"Brother Seraphim planted the melons mentioned in the "The Melon Patch" essay."* As typical with Tom, he then launched into related minutiae… *"Brother had a heavy German accent. He had a sour-puss personality, but had a*

PREP SCHOOL DAYS The Seminary at the University of Notre Dame

good heart. He came from Germany with Brother Boniface who was just the opposite in personality. Both Brothers were hard workers."

Jim Keating offered commentary during the writing phase, but also provided careful editing of several memoires. Jerry Wood sent on a dozen or so of Jim's old Black and white photos (see below).

I emailed a comment to Jim in February, 2011, when the first five essay drafts were in construction, *"I'm beginning to realize that the details of my seminary experiences are perhaps much different than my classmates."* Jim's tongue-in-cheek response was, **"***Remember the advice of an Irish sage: "Don't let the facts get in the way of a good story."*

Jerry Wood, not only a classmate, but later, the chairman at Moreau, offered to read the memoires as they were written. Jerry provided insights on the many Holy Cross events. During April, 2011, following receipt of the first 15 essays, Jerry commented, *"It's wonderful to read these memories of our "Little Sem" years."* Jerry's advice and recollection contributed to the tone and chronology of the memoires.

Jerry forwarded the 50th and 60th anniversary announcements of several of our former Holy Cross resident faculty (teaching priests). He also sent on some of Jim Keating's black and white photos of our Holy Cross fellow students from the mid-1950's. Several of the photos are found in "PREP SCHOOL DAYS."

Andrew Stevans

HOLY CROSS SEMINARY AT THE UNIVERSITY OF NOTRE DAME: CLASS OF 1955

CLASS MOTTO: *"What is taught we learn; what may be found we seek; what may be prayed for we ask of God."*

BACK: Norm Lakatos, Jon Lullo, Jim Keating*, Rog Sowala*, Mike Gelven, Dave Gibson*, Jim Callahan*, Tom Norris*, Dick Cavanaugh, Jude McCusker*, Ron Vogel*, Don Kaiser*

FRONT: Andy Stevans, Lee Skinner*, Bob Kuker*, Jerry Wood*, Tom Hayes*, Fr. Leonard Banas, Fr. Larry LeVasseur, Fr. Harold Riley, Fr. Dean O'Donnell, Don Parks, Jim Glaza, Dick Howard, Ed Whelan*

NOTE: Many Holy Cross graduates including many of the class of 1955(*) attended the University of Notre Dame.

PREP SCHOOL DAYS The Seminary at the University of Notre Dame

NOTRE DAME: INDEX BY NAME (Page 1 of 3)
(Multiple mentions of a name in an essay are listed only once.)

Algeo, Jim	41, 91
Amata, SND, Sr. Mary	49
Ayo CSC, Nick	146
Banas, CSC, Leonard	36, 53, 96, 169
Berry, John	102
Biallas, Leonard	127
Blantz, CSC, Tom	169
Boudreaux, Duane	10, 100
Brennan, Coach Terry	101
Brinker, CSC, Bill	52, 58, 96, 103, 113
Bufalini, Carl	22p, 95
Burtchaell CSC, Jim	146
Butler, John	93, 102
Cadieux, Dick	22p
Callahan, Jim	26, 30, 76, 99, 102, 109, 117p, 118, 125, 129, 161p, 170
Cavanaugh, Dick	26, 30, 119, 129
Collins CSC, John	146
Corcoran CSC, Wendell	8p
Counihan, Bob	81
Chavez, Charlie	22p
Coyne, John	38, 93
Croston CSC, John	161p
Davis, Tom	7
Donovan, Eddie	46
Doyle, Ed	19, 90
Fiedler, CSC, J. Harry	25p, 34, 42, 52, 58, 72, 82, 94, 103, 149, 152p, 162
Gelven, Mike	30, 48, 76, 97p, 109, 118
Gibson, Dave	53, 113, 118, 125, 129, 161p, 167
Gilligan, Jack	161p
Gorman, Tom	143
Glaza, Jim	22p, 23, 30, 48, 75, 113, 125, 137, 151
Grimm CSC, Richard	146
Guglielmi, Ralph	101
Hart, Leon	166
Hayes, John	23, 38

Hayes, Tom	10, 23, 30, 38, 48, 56p, 64, 75p, 161p, 170
Henke, Conrad	131
Hines, Ed	22p, 132
Hornung, Paul	101, 103
Houk, George	19
Howard, Dick	129
Kaiser, Don	28, 97p, 129
Keating, Jim	23, 30, 97p, 102, 105, 109, 113, 131, 161p, 171
Klouda, Bill	2, 33p, 102, 119, 121, 155
Knoll, Jerry, CSC	152p, 154
Kolerman, CSC, Chuck	9
Kovalik, Dick	97p
Krush, Harry	30, 113
Kuker, Bob	54, 56p
Lakatos, Norm	23, 53
Lattner, Johnny	101
Leahy, Coach Frank	101
LeMasse, Ed	62
LeVasseur, CSC, Larry	37, 40, 46, 78
Lullo, Jon	22p, 30, 53, 57, 71, 97p, 102, 109, 113, 118
Lyons, CSC, William	83
Manale, Bernie	47,
Marciano, Rocky	164
Martin CSC, Father	146
Massart, John	58
Matheny, Gerry	75p, 116, 117p
McAuliffe, CSC, Bill	32
McCusker, Jude	113, 129
Mortier, Maurice	16
Mulkerin, Lawrence	37, 155
Murphy, John	131
Norris, Bill	161p
Norris, Tom	22p, 23, 53, 71, 75p, 81, 93, 102, 113, 118, 129, 161p
Novak, Mike	145
O'Donnell, CSC, Dean	45, 85, 90, 99, 143
Panchot, Dan	131
Parks, Don	129
Quirk CSC, Gerry	146
Polumbo, Sam	103

PREP SCHOOL DAYS The Seminary at the University of Notre Dame

Reyes, Hank	40
Riley, CSC, Harold	31, 52, 118, 122, 135p, 143
Roering, Andy	41p, 113, 125
Seraphim CSC, Brother	3, 155
Sandonato CSC, Pete	152p, 162
Schott, Joe	30, 93, 101, 102, 125,148p, 151
Shea, CSC, Ed	78
Sheehan, Gerry	131
Simmons, CSC, William	52, 76, 78, 102, 110, 146, 153, 169
Skinner, Lee	28, 30, 87, 113, 120, 137, 138, 141
Sowala, Rog	22p, 28, 35, 48, 55, 58, 92, 97p, 99, 102, 109, 118, 153
Speltz, Cy	11, 13p, 15p, 30, 38, 42, 76, 91, 97p, 104, 123, 162
St. Rita, SND, Sister M.	3, 33, 65
Stevans, Andy	26, 41p, 78p, 110, 130, 145p, 148p, 161p
Stevans, Jack	1, 3, 28, 63, 110, 112p, 145,
Stevans, Norm	1, 3, 9, 19, 37, 47, 53, 73, 81, 90, 97, 139,146, 164, 165p
Tomes CSC, Bro Bill	161p, 168
VanWolvlear,CSC, John	45, 88p, 89, 96, 123
Vogel, Ron	30, 71, 79, 93
Walsh CSC, Tom	146
Whelan, Ed	28, 97p, 109, 129
Wilsey, Mike	97p, 109
Wood, Jerry	5, 22, 30, 53, 56p, 81, 99, 102, 109, 118, 129 161p, 171
Zacharia, SND, Sr. Mary	49, 53, 68, 71, 74, 91, 119
Zahradnik, Ray	64, 65, 100, 119

...By Andrew Stevans

BOOKS:
ATLANTIC FLEET
A Navy Man's Sea Stories

COUNTRY LIVIN'
Two City Teens work a Summer on the Farm
(Sub-Title: The Farms of Washington County, PA)

GROWIN' UP
The Way Things Used to be—and Still Ought to be...

PREP SCHOOL DAYS
The Seminary at the University of Notre Dame

THINKING IN PRIVATE
The Past, Present and Future...

WRITING:
ANECDOTAL WRITING
Constructing the Personal Essay
(A PowerPoint presentation)

www.ingramcontent.com/pod-product-compliance
Lightning Source LLC
Chambersburg PA
CBHW071501040426
42444CB00008B/1446